Property Dealer

Learn the art of property trading, find deals and build wealth

By Anthony Dixon

Zepp Media

Zepp Media

First published in the United Kingdom in 2018 by Zepp Media

Copyright © Anthony Dixon 2018

The moral right of the author has been asserted.

All rights reserved. No part of this publication may be reproduced or transmitted in any form without the prior permission in writing of the publisher.

ISBN 978-1-72861-090-0 (paperback)

TABLE OF CONTENTS

About the author Anthony Dixon ... 10
Introduction ... 12
    What is property dealing? ... 12
    Buying vs. deal packaging ... 13
    Property dealing techniques ... 14
Chapter One: Below market value (BMV) property ... 17
    What is below market value (BMV) property? ... 17
    Motivated sellers ... 19
        Sellers with financial difficulties ... 19
        Divorcees or separated couples ... 19
        Tired landlords ... 19
        Inherited property ... 20
        Retired people ... 20
        People just want to move ... 20
Chapter Two: Own your patch ... 21
    Local not national marketing ... 21
    Offline advertising ... 21
        Direct mail ... 22
        Newspaper adverts ... 23
    Online advertising ... 23
        Lead capture website ... 23
        Listings sites ... 24
        Social media ... 24
    Estate agents and auctioneers ... 24
    Using online tools ... 25

Viewing the property	26
Condition analysis	26
The importance of due diligence	28
Chapter Three: Qualifying leads	**30**
Pick up the telephone	30
Lead generation and selling leads	30
Customer relationship management (CRM)	31
Chapter Four: Packaging deals	**32**
Chapter Five: Sourcing a house of multiple occupancy (HMO)	**34**
Chapter Six: Attracting investors	**36**
Networking	36
Creating a buyers list	37
Buyer profiling	37
Deal analysis	38
Chapter Seven: Joint venture (JV)	**39**
Chapter Eight: Avoid mistakes when buying BMV property	**44**
Do your due diligence	44
Check the tenant demand	44
Find motivated sellers	44
Keep it local	45
Know that it is BMV property	45
Don't buy in bad areas	45
Avoid the middleman	45
Find good investment property	46

Avoid money-pits	46
Stick to what you are good at	46
Chapter Nine: Rent to Rent	49
What is Rent to Rent?	49
The benefits of the Rent to Rent system	49
Who is Rent to Rent for?	50
What type of lettings does Rent to Rent offer?	51
What sort of contract is used between the landlord and the Rent to Rent professional?	52
Why would a landlord agree to Rent to Rent?	54
Finding landlords for Rent to Rent	54
Business model	57
Sign up for a redress scheme	58
Data Protection Act	58
Property litigation services	59
What sort of property is desired for Rent to Rent to work?	59
Tenant demand	59
What price should be charged for a room?	60
What kind of 'light refurbishment' is required for the property?	60
Renovating HMO property for Rent to Rent	61
Viewings	61
Running the numbers	62
Making an offer	65
Marketing and advertising rooms	65

Managing tenants	66
Insurance	67
Are there any risks?	68
Look professional	69
Professional email	69
Online presence	69
Business cards	69
Call-answering service	70
Chapter Ten: Lease options trading	71
What are lease options?	71
Regulation of lease options	72
How to make lease options work	73
Motivated seller	74
An asset	74
A written agreement	74
The fee	75
Purchase price	75
Timeframe	76
Line up a buyer	77
Purchase options	78
Sandwich options	79
Cooperative options	80
What skills will you need?	81
How to find motivated sellers	83
Lease options in cases of separated and divorced couples	83

Lease options in cases where there are owners in financial difficulty	84
How to market to motivated sellers	84
Calling a vendor with a house for sale	87
Calling a vendor with a house for rent	88
Sourcing property from an estate agent	89
Taking a look at the property	89
Dealing with objections	91
Rent to buy	91
Avoiding problems	93
Chapter Eleven: Buying repossessed property	96
What is the meaning of 'repossession'?	96
What happens once a property is repossessed?	96
How does a lender obtain possession?	96
The repossession process	98
The ethical issues of buying repossessed property	99
Where to find a repossessed property?	100
Getting information from estate agents	100
Getting information from auctioneers	101
Reading the local newspapers	101
Online sources	102
The statistics for repossessions in the UK	103
Research	103
Price analysis	104
Choosing your location	104
Finding a bargain	106

Choosing a property	106
Create the checklist	106
View the property	107
Get expert advice	108
Neighbourhood research	108
Home information pack	109
Survey	109
Sourcing repossessed property	111
Buying at auction	111
Buying through an estate agent	113
Conveyancing	115
What happens when somebody moves in?	117
Safety inspection of the property	118
Inspections for landlords	119
Utilities and services	120
Local authorities	121
Issues with living in a repossessed property	122
Updating details held by credit agencies	122
Dealing with debt collectors	123
The Data Protection Act	124
The Freedom of Information Act	124
Chapter Twelve: Assisted sales	125
Chapter Thirteen: Business structure	128
Accounts and tax	128
The office setup	128
Will I require any staff?	129

Property manager	129
Chapter Fourteen: Managing a refurbishment	131
Planning	131
Records and receipts	131
Add value	132
Buy refurbish refinance	133
Chapter Fifteen: Putting a team together	135
Your legal team	135
Your finance team	136
Your refurbishment team	136
Your sales team	137
Your management team	138
Chapter Sixteen: Tax treatment for a property dealer	139
Chapter Seventeen: Resources	142
Tools to source property deals and conduct analysis	142
Useful sites to source repossessed property	142
Further learning for Rent to Rent	142
Further learning for lease options	144
Further learning by Anthony Dixon	144
Useful sites to help you put together your property dealing team	144
Appendix I Sample lead form	146
Appendix II Example buy to let analysis	149

About the author Anthony Dixon

I have been interested in residential property investment since owning my first property back in 2006. Since then I have read and adopted many techniques to source property around my local region of Derbyshire. I didn't make much money from property in the early days as I did not learn the strategies used by traders and developers to find good deals.

What I have learnt from my experience sourcing property for investment is that it is not easy. What I have put together in this guide is no get rich quick idea. It is simple techniques that can be used with hard work and a methodical approach. What I realised when I started to look for property worth my investment is that you have to do the legwork. You have to get out there and view properties nearly every day. You might even have to view a property several times.

From there you've then got to do your due diligence, which this guide will talk you through in terms of analysing a deal. I have mostly sourced property as an investor on my own as a sole trader, rather than sourcing deals for other investors. My strategy has mainly focused on sourcing below market value property in my local area.

I have learnt from other investors about various techniques that you can use that I have not done myself but may suit you. Every person is different and will have their own methods of working which is why I wanted to put as many ideas in this book on how you can make deals in the residential property market.

I have relied on tried and traditional methods by searching for property through property portals, estate agents and auctioneers. Having spoken to other investors and conducted research on other methods I decided to include them in the book. Some of these ideas may suit the sort of person who has had a sales or marketing background.

One of the aims of being a successful property dealer or investor is to find a motivated seller who may have a suitable property for a deal. This book will show you how to find them and how to structure a deal. I hope my experience and the experience of property traders and investors that I know will help you in your career as a property dealer or investor.

At the time of writing this book, I have been waiting to see the outcome of Brexit before considering sourcing other property for investment. This is has given me the time to put together the information on how to be a property dealer.

Introduction

If you are looking for a book that teaches you about property investment and your run of the mill buy to let and HMO investment then this is not the book for you. This book shows you how to source property for successful property investment or to structure a profitable deal. After reading this book, you will have the knowledge of how to be a successful middleman or how to network for investment.

You may have heard the terms property dealer or property trader bandied about. These people look for houses that they can sell on in the short term. Sometimes they will buy the property or sometimes they may offer the property as packaged deal. Property dealers look to make money on the purchase of a property rather than on the sale, although the financial gains may not be realised until the sale is complete.

What is property dealing?

A property dealer, or property trader, will look for potential deals on residential property rather than commercial property, although it is possible to do both. This book will focus on the residential market as the commercial property market is far more complex and would require a book all to itself. Property dealers will source property from motivated sellers at a discount price that offers a buyer potential gains upon purchase.

Some dealers may purchase the property outright to sell on in the short term to make a profit whereas other dealers may use structured property deal packages without ownership of the property. Both methods can present risk. Usually, dealers will avoid extensive work to properties other than minor refurbishment work and light renovation (a loft-extension to create an extra bedroom is a good example). They are not property developers looking to major building work, nor are they investors that want to hold on to property for many years. Property dealers may use more advanced sourcing techniques other than just trying to find BMV property. They may also specialise in more than one type of trading.

Property dealing suits a professional person who has the time and motivation to look at a lot of properties. They don't need to be sophisticated investors with large sums of wealth and access to finance to buy up properties. Property dealing can be a business that requires just a few thousand pounds to get started depending on whether you want to be a deal-packager. Some traders will have the funds and finance to buy and then sell on quickly. Both approaches to trading property have pros and cons.

Buying vs. deal packaging

I am not going to say either one is better as it is down to each individual, their financial position and their attitude to risk. What I will say is both have different risks that need to be considered. Buying a property will mean you have full control and you won't have the potential of a sale falling through because the vendor of the property (motivated seller) goes back on their word. Any work that you do to the property and pay for is on a property that you own. However, you carry all the risk of covering mortgage payments (assuming you take one) and having capital tied in to the property. Should the venture prove unsuccessful then you could lose a lot of money.

A deal-packager or lease option trader does not need huge amounts of capital and can make a good living structuring deals for a fee. They do not take ownership of the property and have more flexibility as well as the control of the property. The downside of being this kind of trader is that you could lose money if a deal fails to go through or the seller goes back on their word. Money spent on refurbishment and professional fees will be lost and there could be legal problems.

Property dealing techniques

I have structured the book into three parts that I think is a logical order for someone to learn how to become a professional property dealer. Firstly, part one will take you through in detail how us basic sourcing techniques to find motivated sellers. This is an ideal strategy for finding below market value (BMV) property and what I suggest every beginner to property dealing should start with. By starting with these basic techniques you can get to know your area really well and learn how to value property.

From learning the basics, you can then consider using one of the advanced property dealing techniques. I have included in this section strategies such as rent 2 rent, lease option trading, sourcing repossessed property and assisted sales. They carry risk and you should understand that there are legal issues that need to be avoided and I would advise seeking help from a solicitor.

I recommend that you specialise in one other strategy other than sourcing BMV property. Learn the strategy, put into practice and get good at it. Any other leads that you get that may be suitable for another strategy should be passed onto a network of sourcers that you will get to know in time. The final part will teach you how to structure and manage your business.

Part One: Basic Trading Techniques

A property dealer should start off learning as much as they can about their local area. They should assess where the demand for houses is, tenant demand and changes is housing prices. I recommend that a beginner start with the basics of sourcing BMV property and get the experience of doing deals with this kind of property. Once you have had experience and mastered your area, you can then decide on another deal strategy depending on what would suit you.

This section of the book will cover how to find those motivated sellers that can be a lead for BMV property. You will understand the popular advertising techniques that property dealers use to generate leads, both online and offline. The section will then cover how to qualify leads to determine whether you have a potential BMV property. I will explain how you can analyse a property to decide if you have a genuine deal.

Deal packaging will also be covered so that you understand how to structure a deal for a prospective investor, an option you can consider if you don't have the finance to buy yourself. Many dealers earn a living from this method by charging a fee for property sourced that fits what an investor is looking for. Finally, I will discuss how you can seek joint venture in order to build an investment business far quicker than if you invested on your own.

Chapter One: Below market value (BMV) property

What is below market value (BMV) property?

Below market value property is houses and flats that are for sale below the value on the open market. The market value would be what the property would sell for through normal channels like estate agents.

The Royal Institute of Chartered Surveyors (RICS) defines market value as "the estimated amount for which a property should exchange on the date of valuation between a willing buyer and a willing seller in arm's-length transaction after property marketing wherein the parties had each acted knowledgeably, prudently and without compulsion."

Valuing the property involves comparing with other properties in the area and the level of demand which we will cover later in this guide. It is important to know that there are below market value properties that can make you a profit and there are also below market value properties that are money-pits that will cost you a lot to rectify and therefore are bought at the true value.

Investors and dealers can use various marketing techniques to source property in local areas for considerably less than the market value. Anyone looking for below market value will be aiming for a substantial discount, typically 20-25 percent BMV. There are professionals who can achieve more than this but it is rare. It is important to remember that lower-priced properties are more suitable for your search for discounted property. You are more likely to find people in financial difficulties who own cheaper properties. It is possible that you will find a seller with a mid-high value property and I have included a chapter about sourcing HMO property as another target market but don't expect to get many deals. Ideally, the business marketing should concentrate on below market value at the cheaper end of the market. Typical properties will be your terraced townhouses that are of older age (usually Victorian age) with two to three bedrooms. Flats are also a possibility but there will not be many in the lower price bracket. The value range for sought-after properties would be in the range of up to £125,000 if the property were sold on the market.

You are not going to be marketing in areas where there are large expensive houses that may be more suitable for other investing techniques. To get enough leads for your business you are going need to be operating your business in a big enough area. The numbers of houses that are suitable for sourcing below market value are your stock. If you are living in a village or small town there might not be enough stock to generate enough leads for your business. You might want to consider operating your business somewhere else and you might even have to consider moving. You probably need a stock of 50,000 houses to market to.

Sourcing BMV property can be an excellent way to generate an income by selling leads or, with experience, packaging deals. Finding motivated sellers would also be an extremely effective strategy if you are an investor and intend to buy BMV property for yourself. You can also use BMV property as an incentive for other investors to form a joint venture with you.

Motivated sellers

Motivated sellers are the little golden nuggets that you are looking for in your search for below market value property. Motivated sellers will be keen to sell a property and are going to be more likely to sell the property below the market value in order to shift the burden. Each motivated seller will have different reasons for selling a property quickly. Sometimes they are termed 'distressed sellers' because they are in a difficult situation that may be causing emotional stress as well as financial problems.

Sellers with financial difficulties

There are going to be sellers that are in difficult financial situations and are struggling with mortgage payments or have other substantial debts. Changes in circumstances such as a change in career or redundancy could lead to somebody experiencing great stress and wants out of the property quickly.

Divorcees or separated couples

A couple either married or not, may have taken out a joint mortgage on a property but in time their relationship has broken down. One or both has moved out leaving a financial mess that both will want to end quickly. The mortgage payments and the upkeep of the property will be a burden and will be a prime reason for a quick sale.

Tired landlords

There are going to be property owners who have been renting their property out to tenants but have become tired of managing the property. Managing a property and dealing with tenants is not for everyone and can become quite stressful. Problems with maintenance, late rent payments and constant complaints from tenants can all take its toll on a landlord. They may have decided that enough is enough and it is time to sell up and want a quick sale. This is most likely the case when a landlord has experienced a bad tenant.

Inherited property
Perhaps a property of a recently deceased person has been passed down to the next generation. The new owner doesn't want to move in or become a landlord and wants to sell up. The property may have repair issues and has become a burden to the new owner and is sitting empty. This is a good opportunity for a discounted property.

Retired people
There may be elderly owners who are moving into residential homes or to homes that have better facilities for people who have mobility issues. They may have a house that they want to sell quickly so they can use the cash for their retirement home or for their care.

People just want to move
There will be some people that will just want to move rather than be in a desperate financial situation. It may be because they have made a career change or their job requires them to relocate. It could be that the seller wants to move closer to their family.

Chapter Two: Own your patch

Local not national marketing

Anybody starting out in their search for below market value property should start with their local area. You need to build up an understanding of how the local property market works and what the average price for a certain property in an area should be. That way you know what sort of price you are looking to offer to a motivated seller. It is likely that when you start out you are going to be a one-man band and you won't have the people, resources and money to do a nationwide marketing campaign. Plus, it will take you a lot longer to research areas across the country gauging how properties are priced and what sort of discount you can achieve.

By focusing on your area you are going to start knowing the difference between the prices of two bedroomed houses compared to three bedroom houses on any street or area. You will know the difference in price between houses in good condition compared with a property that needs refurbishing. You can't run a successful business if you can't distinguish these differences in prices. I believe you have two routes to source local property. Firstly, using marketing to generate leads (motivated sellers). Secondly, using traditional methods of analysing property sold through estate agents and auction houses.

Offline advertising

There are two main marketing techniques to use to search for below market value property, direct mail and newspaper adverts.

Direct mail

Your first task in order to produce an effective and co-ordinated leaflet campaign is to buy a map of your local area. You require a map that has details of every street in your town or city. Your job is to then mark out areas on the map where there is suitable low-cost housing. Areas where you are going to find cheaper townhouses on long streets of terraced housing and narrow roads. Once you have marked these areas out with borders you then know which streets to do your leaflet drops.

You should do the drops for each area about once every two-three months. One week you do one area the next week you do another area and so on. The average response is going to be low and it can take time to build awareness of your business. Statistics show that it can take seven leaflet drops to the same house before a prospective customer will call your business. The main aim of the leaflets is to get known in the area as people can pass on details to others who may be in a situation where they need help.

The other form of direct mail is targeted sales letters. When you are dropping leaflets around houses, make a note of properties that may look empty. They may have a 'for sale' board up and have no visible furnishings in the front room. Make a note of the street and the house number as you continue making your way around with your leaflets. You can find out the name of the owner of the property using the Land Registry. All you need is the postcode, which you can find out online, and the address and it will cost you just £1 to get the name on the deeds. You now have a lead that you can post a more personal and targeted to letter to. Your letter can explain your business and that you are a solution provider for people who are struggling to sell their property.

You may want to employ someone on a casual basis to do your leaflet drop, which is fine, but make sure they are doing the job. It may be wise to just be on site around the streets whilst they are doing the drops to keep an eye on them. Give them instructions to make a note on houses that may be empty.

Newspaper adverts
Advertising in your local newspaper is an effective but expensive way to advertise your business. You can place the ad in the classified section of the paper under the 'property wanted' heading. The advert will need an enticing headline like the leaflet to encourage sellers to contact you. The advert should include your mobile or landline phone number. You should advertise your business as local with words like 'local investors ready to buy' The advertising can cost around £50 for a two-week publication so this will be an expensive form of advertising if done on a regular basis.

Online advertising
You can use a mixture of online marketing methods to generate leads.

Lead capture website
One crucial and effective method of generating consistent leads into your business is to have a lead capture website. This is a landing page that you can use to capture the contact details of motivated sellers. The landing page should have a form that a seller can submit their contact information and a few details about the property (location, type of property, number of

bedrooms. With a well-crafted landing page that is search engine optimised (SEO) along with pay per click advertising (SEM), you will start generating leads. You may want to consult someone who knows a lot about SEO and SEM and make sure it is optimised for your local area. You can outsource all of this by using freelancing sites like Fiverr and Upwork.

Listings sites
By putting out daily adverts on sites like Gumtree you can build awareness of your business and start gathering leads. The advert will need a link to your lead capture landing page. The adverts should be placed regularly for this advertising to be effective.

Social media
You can use paid advertising on social media sites like Facebook. A bit like managing a pay-per-click campaign, you can target your social media adverts by certain demographics such as age, location and earnings. You may want to keep your budget low to start with and see what adverts work and analyse the results. If the adverts are generating conversions (person fills out your form on the landing page) then you can put more money into the advertising campaign.

Estate agents and auctioneers
You may be able to find good deals direct from agents and auctioneers. Some properties will be repossessions and empty and the owner will be looking for a quick sale. You can use online tools to filter through potential properties that would make a good deal. It is possible to buy a property from an auction catalogue before the auction takes place if you make a

suitable offer around the guide price. Establishing relationships with estate agents will help you to find good deals. Just remember not to waste their time, if you say that you are interested in a property then make sure you line up an investor to purchase. Failing to complete on a purchase is going irritate them and they won't want to do business with you in the future.

Estate agents and letting agents can be an excellent source of due diligence and give you an expert opinion on housing prices, rental prices and tenant demand.

Using online tools

I am going to show you how you can use a property portal's tools to filter through properties in your local area. By using these tools you can find properties that might be a possible lead for a below market value property. Zoopla and Rightmove are two portals that have tools that you can use to filter and find potential properties on the market from a motivated seller. I have a video on my YouTube channel, *Dixon Property Deals,* on how you can use a property portal to find these kinds of properties.

You should be looking for properties that might be priced lower for the same type such as a two bedroomed terraced house. You can use the portal's tools to filter by property type and price. You can then select the order by how long they have been on the market, whether there have been any price reductions.

You can also use websites like Mouseprice.com to find sold house prices for properties in your area. This will give you a history of the sales for similar properties which you can use to value a property. By using these online tools you can start to filter those properties that are worth viewing and save you time. You may have to look at hundreds of properties in your area before you have enough experience to know your valuations and spot a good deal.

Viewing the property

When viewing the property you should look around at everything and use your sense of smell just like any investor would. You are searching for possible repairs and problems with the property. But you should be making notes on what work is required to get the property ready for sale or letting. When you have completed your viewing you should have a checklist of things that are okay and things that need rectifying. From this, you can start to work out your costings as part of your deal analysis.

Remember, the money is made on the purchase, not the sale. You should be working out what the maximum sales price could be and work back from the price you can pay for the property plus the cost of works and subtract from the sales price. From that, you will work out how much profit is left and whether you have a good deal. There are other aspects involved in a deal analysis which I will explain in Chapter Six Attracting Investors. It may be that the property is an absolute wreck and spending the money to fix it will simply leave no profit. If this is the case it is better to walk away.

Condition analysis

As you get to know your area, the types of property and the changes in price according to condition you can start to do some research and analysis. The analysis will then give you a guideline for what sort of price you can achieve on a property. Below is an example of how you can research properties in your area. Remember you are looking for lower value property in working-class areas.

Example of house prices in a neighbourhood

	Two bedroom terraced	Three bedroom terraced	Three bedroom Semi-detached
Refurbishment	£78,000	£85,000	£105,000
Tired rental	£89,000	£95,000	£115,000
First-rate	£95,000	£100,000	£125,000

By using this table as your system you can classify properties and become proficient in valuing property. You will be looking for two bedroomed terraced and three bedroomed terraced properties as well as the odd three bedroom semi-detached house. These types of property are what you are likely to find in your working-class neighbourhoods where properties are likely to be of Victorian age.

A refurbishment is a property that requires a lot of work doing to it in order to get the property ready for the market. This could include kitchen, bathroom, carpets, painting and decoration. A tired rental is a property that doesn't require a lot of work, maybe just a lick of paint to spruce it up. A first-rate is a property that is in pristine condition, well decorated with every room looking immaculate. You can start doing your research by talking to estate agents and letting agents and using online tools to look at past sold prices and the prices of similar properties.

You should use one table for one estate or area that you have bordered on the map of your local town. This area might be around 5-10 streets in a neighbourhood. From your research, you will get an idea of the differences in price for each type of property. So a three bedroomed terraced house might be priced at £85,000 for a property in need of refurbishment, £95,000 for a tired rental property and £100,000 for a first-rate property. You need to know your numbers so that you can spot deals quickly.

The importance of due diligence

Due diligence is crucial if you are to find a successful property deal. Don't just rely on looking at properties online and think that you have a deal. You have to get out there and visit estate agents and letting agents. Talk to them and find out what the most popular locations in your area are and what kind of property is sought after. You have to view property and look at the differences in condition. Work out how much it would cost to refurbish a property to get it to the maximum value. How much will it cost? How much profit will be left after the work?

Sometimes you think you may have a deal when you see a heavily discounted property. But when you factor in the cost of the work to get the property in good condition there may not be much profit left. You basically don't have a deal; you have just bought the property at its true value. Using alternative channels to find a property to buy can result in a lot more problems and failures than buying through your retail channel such as estate agents. Therefore, it is very important that you take your time and do your due diligence. Money is to be made but be careful and seek advice where you can.

Chapter Three: Qualifying leads

Pick up the telephone

Once you are getting responses from your various advertising efforts you now have what we call leads. Leads are the lifeblood of your business and without them, you have no business. You want leads coming in every day, every week if you want to be successful. When you have the contact details of the lead you should ring them as soon as possible. It is important to be prepared for the phone call.

The best way to prepare for the call is to have a paper form with a list of questions and spaces for answers. I have included an example of a form that you can use to ask the questions you need to know to qualify the lead. By qualifying the lead you know whether you have a genuinely motivated seller that would agree to a discount deal.

Lead generation and selling leads

Those who are starting outsourcing BMV property may want to consider setting up a lead generation business. A lead generation business can be an excellent way to start out before moving to the next level such as property investment or deal packaging. There is also the possibility that some leads won't work for you and you may want to pass those leads onto another dealer or investor. You might get leads for HMO property, serviced accommodation commercial property and land which may not be the kind of investment opportunity you are looking for.

Customer relationship management (CRM)

As the leads start to come in from your various marketing activities you may want to think about organising your customer relationship management. It will be easy to forget about the particular details of each seller, especially if you are talking to several sellers every day. You can use CRM software to help you manage all of this information, recording all the information from your seller lead form. This way you are organised and you can get the information up in front of you to remind you where you are in your negotiation and the deal process.

There is free software available online such as Zoho CRM, which is a good option when you are starting out and you have a small budget as it is free. You could think about using more advanced cloud software such as Salesforce as your business grows.

Chapter Four: Packaging deals

Once you have qualified your lead and you have a motivated seller willing to sell at 25 percent BMV then you can put together a deal for another investor. This is known as deal packaging. We will talk about how to find investors in the next chapter. Let's say that you have an interested investor but doesn't want a hands-on experience whilst buying the property. You now have the opportunity to structure a deal.

How much you charge for the deal package will depend on how much you put into the deal. You can expect to charge anything from £1000 (your minimum fee) to £5000, depending on what work you put into it. Many dealers will offer a package that goes through the whole buying process, from making the offer to completion of the sale. You should think about putting together a tier of charges for each stage that you involved with.

So for just introducing the investor to the seller that results in an offer you receive £1000. Alternatively, for introducing the parties, arranging the finance (with a mortgage broker), arranging the conveyancing, getting quotes for refurbishing, completing the refurbishment and completion of the sale you could charge up to £5000. Your charges may also be affected by the value of the property, so you could charge more on a property worth £100,000 compared to a property of £70,000.

To offer deal packages you are going to need a team of specialists that you can call on to help the sale go through to completion. You are going to need:

- A conveyancer or specialist property lawyer
- A mortgage broker
- Builder and specialist tradesmen (electricians, plumbers, heating engineers)
- Other property dealers (for deals that may not suit you)
- Surveyor or valuation expert (if you cannot value a property yourself)

When presenting your packaged deal you will want to produce pdf or print off the information as a brochure for potential buyer and investors. The information should include the value of the property, photos of the interior and exterior of the property, details of what the property includes, what improvements are required and what work you, as the dealer, will be doing. It is going to be similar to the kind of brochure or pdf that an estate agent would present to you for a property for sale. The only difference will be that you will also include details on the fees that you will charge for your work.

A professional document will also include figures for deal analysis that I will explain in Chapter Six Attracting Investors. Deal packaging will not suit every investor and you will need to find those that are looking for a hands-off investment. Professional investors will want to cut out the middleman, avoid sourcing fees and do their own due diligence. They will oversee the project from purchase to completion and get the property ready for sale or let.

Chapter Five: Sourcing a house of multiple occupancy (HMO)

When starting your business you should just focus on cheaper property rather than HMO and large properties. The reason is that it is a numbers game and for every 100 properties that you look at, either from your desktop or by viewing, you may only find ten or twenty properties that are a good deal. There is going to be less housing stock if you are considering sourcing HMO properties. There will also be less interest as HMO property is expensive and only attainable for wealthy and sophisticated investors rather than your small investor that wants a buy to let for extra income or a pension.

Just remember that you going to have extra costs when running an HMO so as part of your presentation of an HMO a deal you should include estimations for:

- HMO landlord insurance
- Cleaner for communal areas at least
- Utilities including gas, electricity and water
- Council Tax
- Broadband (a must for student rentals)
- TV Licensing
- Potential management fees

It is important to know how many rooms need to be let to break even which should also be presented to investors. You are going to have to look at the standard of rooms by viewing a potential property. Are they up to standard compared to other HMO properties on the street? HMO property is becoming increasingly sophisticated so you may need to think about installing flat-screen TVs and high-speed fibre optic broadband. Refurbishing the property to a high spec may cost more but could lead to fewer voids and more profit in the long-term. These are important parts of a deal that you need to think about. The property will need to be legally in good safe condition so gas certificates, five-year electrical condition reports and licensing will need to be paid for and passed. To complete a successful deal the property should be earning £1000 profit per month.

HMO is a cash-flow property investment strategy so the margins are crucial. If an investor is not convinced that the property can achieve good profit margins then you are not going to sell a deal. As I have already said about due diligence, it is crucial to talk to estate agents and letting agents in the area. Take your time to find out about tenant demand which is going to be very important for the success of the multi-let property. Voids are more common with HMOs so you want lots of interest in your rooms.

Chapter Six: Attracting investors

Networking

You are going to need a network of buyers if you want deals to happen. By networking with local property investors, developers and landlords you should establish some relationships and contacts. When you get a lead from a motivated seller you want to have this pool of contacts ready to purchase the property. You can attend networking events such as the Progressive Property Network (PPN) or the Property Investors Network (PIN).

They are a local get together held every month for investors to network and build relationships. There are also business events held by the Chambers of Commerce in your town or city. These events will provide you with useful contacts including interested investors, business people and services. There is also likely to be events held for local landlords organised by the National Landlord's Association. This could be an opportunity to find tired landlords.

When attending networking events it is important not to push things too fast when talking to potential investors. Just casually state what you do and how you are willing to help investors find property in your local area. Let them know the areas where you advertise and source property. The kind of property you source will be suitable for refurbish to sell investors and buy to let landlords. You don't directly sell at the networking event you just want to let people know what you do and what you want in property investment.

Networking doesn't have to just about socialising at events and meetings you can also use the internet to network with interested investors. You can use professional social media such as LinkedIn to find interested investors for your deals. When you have contacted and established a relationship with the investor you can invite them to your group where you can post deals.

You can also set up a group on Facebook to post your latest deals. You can also use online forums to build relationships with investors. By using your knowledge and being helpful on the forum you can start to establish yourself as a trustworthy source of property. You will have to research the internet to find forums that would be relevant to you and your location.

Creating a buyers list

By using some of the same techniques to market to motivated sellers you can build a buyers list. Building a landing page and channelling your advertising on social media, pay-per-click, SEO and listings could help you build an extensive list of buyers looking for discounted property in your area. You may want to entice buyers to fill out your form on the landing page by offering a free report or a list of properties you are currently offering as a deal. You should start building your buyers list as soon as you start marketing to motivated sellers. You need buyers ready to call upon as soon as you have a lead or a potential deal.

Buyer profiling

We have already talked about CRM when organising your sales process and it might be worth organising your data for buyers. You can profile your potential investor by the amount they are willing to spend, the type of property they are looking for, whether they want a property ready to let or are looking for a refurbishment and what location. This will help you save time and find the buyers that will be most interested in the lead from a motivated seller. You don't want to waste people's time to try to present leads and deals that you know the investor will be interested in.

Deal analysis

We have talked about deal packaging and presenting the deal as a pdf or brochure for the potential buyer. If the property is to be sold to an investor then you should include some deal analysis in your marketing materials. You should include what sort of yield can be achieved from the rental of the property. Your yield will be calculated as the annual rent achieved as a percentage of the property value.

For HMO property, you may want to include the estimated bills for the property as well as the yield achieved from maximum occupancy. Most experienced investors will know that the potential yield is not always likely due to void periods of occupancy.

You can use spreadsheet software such as Microsoft Excel to analyse deals including computations on discount (BMV), rent, yield, costs, finance (deposits, loans and mortgages), the rate of interest, re-mortgaging, cash required to cover mortgage payments, return on investment and exit points. I have included an example of a deal analysis spreadsheet for a buy to let deal.

Chapter Seven: Joint venture (JV)

Through your various networking activities, you may come across opportunities to invest in property through a joint venture. This is an excellent strategy to invest in property if you have only a little cash but lots of time. There is no better time than the present to seek joint venture investments as interest rates provide little return for investors' savings.

An investor will be looking for opportunities to make their money work for them but may have little time to source properties and oversee a project. As you are already sourcing properties that are potential refurbish for profit opportunities then you already have something to pitch to an investor.

By having the time to search through hundreds of properties and finding deals you already have something to bring to the table. In exchange, you can tap into their wealth and access to finance that perhaps you may struggle to obtain if you invested on your own.

According to Wikipedia, a joint venture can be defined as,

"A **joint venture** (**JV**) is a business entity created by two or more parties, generally characterized by shared ownership, shared returns and risks, and shared governance. Companies typically pursue joint ventures for one of four reasons: to access a new market, particularly emerging markets; to gain scale efficiencies by combining assets and operations; to share risk for major investments or projects; or to access skills and capabilities."

There will be many investors that want to get into property investment for the first time as they see other investments failing or enduring volatility such as businesses and stock markets. You can position yourself as a professional with expertise in sourcing and investing in below market value residential property.

By offering investors the potential for instant gains in equity from a BMV property you will have no trouble in getting interest. A joint venture will suit property that is in need of refurbishment where value can be added with a substantial profit margin left on the sale value. Investors may not be looking for a long-term buy to let investment but this should be considered as a backup exit strategy should the property struggle to sell or does not generate the desired profit initially.

Tapping into joint venture investment could see you building up a property business much quicker as you increase your buying power. There are different ways to structure the joint venture depending on what each party brings to the project. Here are some of the ways you can structure a JV.

A straight JV is formed where one party has the time to put into sourcing the property and overseeing to completion. The other party has the money to invest and the access to finance. The partner with the cash will be looking for someone that they can get along with.

An intellectual property JV is where one party as skills and knowledge that can be proven with a track record. Another party may be interested in the joint venture based on tapping into the other party's skill and ability.

A deed of trust venture is where the JV partner that has the funds takes ownership of the mortgage, so in effect, they are not lending the money out. This reduces the cash-rich investors risk if they have reservations. A deed of trust is basically a contract between parties so that there is a share of equity, rental profits and losses. What percentage of that share goes to each party will depend on what each party puts into the venture.

A tenants-in-common JV is where the partners take 50 percent ownership on the title deeds sharing the risk and reward equally. Both parties need to be aware that their credit reports are linked by the venture and should keep everything clean to avoid problems obtaining future finance. This venture structure will suit partners who have equal expertise and finance.

You can network and find investors of different types from angel investors, private investors, venture capitalists, friends and family. But whomever you decide to go into business within a joint venture you should make sure there are proper legal agreements. Disputes, falling outs and legal action can be common and it would be an even worse situation if it is with a member of your own family.

Angel investors, private investors and venture capitalists are professional and will demand greater returns and control. But they will have a lot of experience and good contacts that will improve the chances of the venture being a success.

Friends, family, solo-entrepreneurs and opportunists are not professional investors and may take more time and effort to persuade them to invest. They will want regular communication and will worry a lot more about their money. They may demand less return on investment as long as you beat the banks where they will never exceed five percent interest. With current interest rates, you will have no trouble in persuading them on this aspect of a deal.

As when looking for investors to pitch a deal do not directly sell to investors rather state that you are looking for a joint venture. They may not be interested themselves but may refer you to someone that would be interested. Being too pushy may put somebody off; hard selling really does not work. Below is a script that you can use to introduce yourself to a potential investor.

"Hello, I'm Joe Bloggs. I'm a local property sourcer (trader, dealer or investor - whichever title you prefer); I help people who are in financial difficulty and I invest in property professionally. I'm looking to help more people out of financial difficulty. Do you know anybody who may need help? I'm also looking to help local investors get an excellent return on their investment through Joint Venture arrangements. Do you know anyone who might want an excellent return on their money?"

Your talks and negotiations with prospective investors should be on a one-to-one basis away from networking events. This is when you can have your serious discussions about potential business opportunities. You have got to build the relationship; investors will not just jump into a deal. Establishing a relationship with people you already know is obviously going to be easier but establishing a relationship with new people you network with will take time. By letting them know what you do without hard selling and getting to know their aims, wants and interest you will start to establish a mutual interest that will suit a joint venture.

Chapter Eight: Avoid mistakes when buying BMV property

Whether you are buying for yourself, sourcing for an investor or are part of an investment group you should make sure that you have a deal. Below is a summary of what this guide has taught you:

Do your due diligence

I know I have mentioned this already but it is the most important phase of sourcing BMV property. You need the evidence that the property has profit potential, to convince yourself or interested investors. Use the techniques I have included such as online property tools and property viewings and speaking to estate agents and property professionals who know your area.

Check the tenant demand

You may be looking at a property as a refurbish to sell or refinance but you should still make sure that you check the rental demand. The property might not sell quickly so it is best to have a plan B. Most investors look to buy to let as a backup strategy if the property has a lack of interest or if it doesn't generate the profit that was hoped.

Find motivated sellers

Use the online tools like Zoopla along with marketing activities to find motivated sellers. They are going to be more open to lower offers. This is where you can find a good deal.

Keep it local
Become an expert in your area and focus your viewings, analysis and marketing in your local neighbourhoods. It is going to be much easier logistically to view local property rather than driving up and down the country. You can also start to build relationships with local property agents.

Know that it is BMV property
Just because a property appears to be on offer at a discount doesn't mean it actually is. If the property requires a scheme of works that wipes out any potential profit then you don't have a deal.

Don't buy in bad areas
Any areas of your town or city that has a bad reputation due to crime or bad neighbours should not be considered. Even if there are many cheap properties for sale it is likely that you are going to struggle to sell or find a tenant. The demand will not be sufficient for property in these areas.

Avoid the middleman
You will find that there are entrepreneurs and dealers claiming extraordinary discounts on property that you may be interested in. If it truly is a good deal then the dealer or entrepreneur should be looking to buy it themselves. You will also have to pay their commission on top of the purchase price. It is better to source property yourself and conduct your own due diligence so that you know, as certain as you can be, that you are getting a good deal.

Find good investment property
Some properties may not be a good long-term investment. If you are planning on using a buy to let strategy or you sourcing for investors looking to buy to let then you want a property that is going to generate a positive cash flow. Avoid buying property in isolated areas where there is a low demand for tenants. A good investment will at least be able to cover the expenses and costs and appreciate in value in the long term.

Avoid money-pits
Some property will require a hell of a lot of work to get in good condition. You will have to assess whether a large amount of investment in the work is worth it for the profit that might be achieved. A property may appear to be for sale at a substantial discount but will actually result in a loss! It might be worth paying for a surveyor if the property is in a bad state that needs considerable renovation.

Stick to what you are good at
This book has focused on finding cheaper value property but you are likely to come across leads from people who own commercial property, land, serviced accommodation and HMO property. It is best to pass those leads on to other dealers or investors that have the knowledge and skill to make it a worthwhile investment. You can decide to source and invest in this property once you have gained further skills and knowledge through reading, courses and speaking to experienced professionals. But first get good at finding discount property and understand the house pricing and hotspots in your local area.

Part Two: Advanced trading techniques

Before using any of these techniques to structure deals and build your portfolio you must seek advice from a solicitor. Using techniques such as lease options, rent to rent and assisted sales will require written contracts and paperwork to cover the legal side of the deal. Don't look for templates online and think that it will cover everything. A trained professional will be able to discuss with you your exact needs and put together contracts that will help you avoid legal disputes and cover you in the event that there are any.

I suggest that you pick one technique to master alongside your day to day search for BMV property. I have not used lease options or rent to rent but I have used assisted sales, which I think fits well with my search for discounted property in my local city of Derby. Both lease options and rent to rent will have legal issues and I can't vouch for either one of them as being a successful strategy, personally. However, I have included them as options that you could consider and I certainly know of investors that are using these strategies to gain wealth.

Some experts and investors are suggesting that now is a good time to get into rent to rent as many HMO landlords are looking to sell up due to tax changes in Section 24.

Lease options are growing in popularity but it is unknown whether they will become regulated by the government in the future which could affect current trading. Please read through this section of the book and decide what you feel would suit you and your investment goals.

Chapter Nine: Rent to Rent

What is Rent to Rent?

Rent to Rent is a strategy used by a property professional to acquire HMO properties from 'distressed' landlords without buying the property. Landlords who own properties that have become tired and neglected and are difficult to let are a prime target. A guaranteed rent is offered to the landlord with a light refurbishment and long-term contract also agreed. The professional will then let the rooms in the property on an individual basis. The profit generated is the difference between tenants' payments less the rent paid to the landlord and utility bills.

Rent to Rent is a strategy that can build up cash-flow fast where it is possible to be making close to £1000 net per calendar month from the rentals on a single property. Once three or four properties are controlled a significant annual salary can be achieved. A Rent to Rent scheme will be responsible for vetting and managing the tenants and will also oversee the maintenance and repairs to the property.

The benefits of the Rent to Rent system

Although buying an HMO property is a good strategy for generating an income from letting there are barriers to entry for the average investor. A mortgage is required with a 25 percent deposit on the property, planning permission may be also be needed, regulations have to be met and licensing costs need to be paid.

Rent to Rent avoids all of these factors that put up a barrier to entry in the multi-let property market. The only initial outlay will be a light refurbishment to get a property ready for letting rooms to tenants. The business can be started from home with no major overheads to cover. On top of this, you can enjoy a decent cash-flow from each property, even after paying ongoing bills and the landlord or letting agent.

Who is Rent to Rent for?

This guide can be helpful to investors at different stages of their property investment career. You may be considering rent to rent in one of the following situations:

- You have heard about Rent to Rent either in the media, from friends talking about Rent to Rent or investors that you know in your area.
- You already control a property on a Rent to Rent agreement but you are not sure you are on the right track with how you are running your business.
- You are a property investor that already owns rental property and are seeking cash-flow to increase your income.
- You are not sure what business to go into but are thinking about a property investment venture.

Whichever position you are in this guide can help you make a decision on whether rent to rent is a good fit for your investment plans. Even if this rent to rent is not for you then some of the tips in this guide can help you with running another property strategy such as property management, property dealing/sourcing and other letting investments.

What type of lettings does Rent to Rent offer?

This scheme can be used for student lets and working professionals. You could also market the property to those on benefits and low incomes. Which type of let you market to will be based on the quality of the rooms in the property, the location, the rental price of each room and the transport links from the property. Working professionals may want an upmarket décor and be willing to spend more on the rent. They may want city based locations both for commuting to work and nightlife.

Students will want low budget accommodation close to a university or college. If you are marketing to people with low incomes and benefits then I advise strict management and thorough vetting. You may get away with offering basic quality rooms but a low-income tenant may pose more of a risk to neglecting the property.

There are different types of accommodation that rent to rent managers could control such as HMO, single occupancy houses, serviced accommodation and local housing association property. However, this eBook focuses on the HMO market and single occupancy housing (buy to let property). Should you want to explore different properties and markets then you will need further reading.

It is best practice to focus on only one business model. Trying to manage HMO properties as well as serviced accommodation will be stressful as they are very different in how they are managed.

Rent to Rent takes the idea of the corporate let, where a company takes on the rent or lease of a property and then sub-lets to employees, and brings it into the private rented market.

What sort of contract is used between the landlord and the Rent to Rent professional?

A commercial lease contract will usually be drawn up as an agreement between the landlord and the Rent to Rent professional. The contract may differ depending on the route you go to control the property:

Dealing direct with a landlord and taking control of the property

Establishing an agreement with an agent to take control of the property

This will differ from a standard AST contract and will last a longer term, typically five years. There may be break clauses in the contracts, usually every six months, should things go badly wrong to protect both parties. The contract will require a bigger deposit of over two month's rent, three months being a common agreement.

Anyone embarking on a Rent to Rent business should seek the advice of a solicitor who can draw up a professional contract for Rent to Rent schemes. There are solicitors who specialise in property and will help you draw up contract agreements.

You may also want advice on the kind of agreement you want with your tenants and guidance on what to include. It is essential that you have things down in writing not just a handshake on an agreement. You will avoid disputes with landlords, agents, and tenants reducing the need for legal services.

You may also be tempted to use contract templates that can be downloaded for free on the internet. Don't do this, the template may miss important information or may not be a good fit for your arrangement. Always get help from a legal professional to draw up a professional contract agreement, it will put your mind at ease that there isn't anything important left out that could have future repercussions.

Why would a landlord agree to Rent to Rent?

Landlords want a variety of safety nets when they let their property such as no void periods, no missed or late payments, no tenant management, guaranteed start date, the same day of the monthly rent payment, fully vetted and screened tenants, maintenance included and good condition of the property.

Unfortunately, most landlords run into problems when one or several of these safety nets are not achieved. Some landlords maybe 'accidental' and have not had the experience or somebody may be a landlord who has done multi-let but got too involved and found the wrong tenants due to poor vetting.
A Rent to Rent professional provides the solution to landlords who are in trouble with their property providing all the safety nets desired from the letting. The Rent to Rent scheme is essentially a middle-man between the landlord and the tenants.

Finding landlords for Rent to Rent

There are two ways to find landlords who would agree to you taking over the management of a property. The first method is to go straight to landlords through various means of marketing. The second method is to visit letting agents who may agree to a rent to rent arrangement.

A good starting point is to get to know your area really well. If you have experience as a property sourcer or dealer then this will help. By getting to know your patch well you can understand the market better, especially if you want to know what sort of rooms are selling well. By using tools on sites like Zoopla and Rightmove you can filter properties to suit HMO.

You will need to use various advertising to attract the attention of landlords who will get in contact with you should they have a suitable property.

Leaflet drops are a low-cost strategy to start with but this will take time to generate leads. You will need to drop leaflets in the same areas every three months. It can take seven leaflet drops to the same person before there is a response. This is due to trust.

Newspapers are another traditional strategy for advertising your business. The best place for the advert will be in the classified section. The advert should contain a quick message along with a contact phone number.

Radio advertising can be effective for your local area but will be expensive. In terms of getting your business out there, it is a good marketing strategy.

Networking at local landlord meetings would be an excellent method of getting your business known to potential clients.

All of these are traditional methods of advertising your service but the cheapest and best starting point would be to contact your local council. Your local council will have a list of all the HMO properties in the area and the landlords who own them. The lists will have the contact details of each landlord. By getting through to the right department at your local council and asking politely they should pass on those details.

If you want to avoid sourcing property and finding landlords yourself then you can use the services of a professional property sourcer or dealer. They will expect a fee of around £1000-£5000 should you come to an agreement with the landlord and take control of the HMO property. This is an expensive option but does take out a lot of the legwork and time wasted on unsuitable properties or uncooperative landlords.

Establishing a relationship with agents may be tricky and will require many visits to become well-known and build trust. When you first visit and chat with an agent you should make sure you leave a business card and marketing materials with the key decision maker. Should the agent have a suitable property be sure to talk to the key decision maker to discuss your service. You should be trying to establish a relationship where the agent continues there normal contract with the landlord but instead of looking for tenants they sign a commercial lease agreement with your business. The next page shows how it works:

Business model

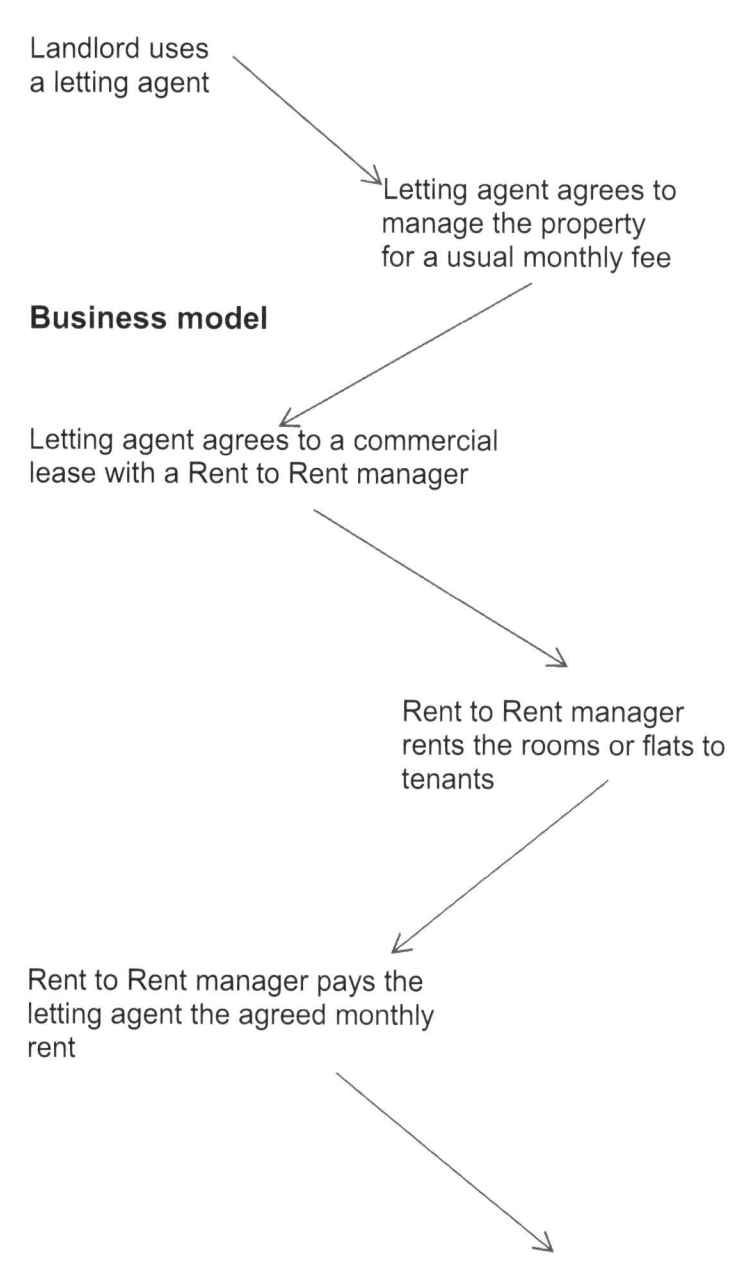

Landlord uses a letting agent

↘ Letting agent agrees to manage the property for a usual monthly fee

↙ Letting agent agrees to a commercial lease with a Rent to Rent manager

↘ Rent to Rent manager rents the rooms or flats to tenants

↙ Rent to Rent manager pays the letting agent the agreed monthly rent

↘ Agent pays the landlord the monthly rent minus the monthly management fee

Sign up for a redress scheme

To help build credibility with landlords and agents and give an image of professionalism it is important to sign up to a redress scheme. This shows that you are a regulated professional service like any other property manager or letting agent. Your business has to perform to standards set by the scheme.

The Property Ombudsman
This website will help to resolve any complaints made by landlords or tenants. The site provides free and impartial advice for the resolution of disputes. The service provides a detailed guideline on complaints procedures and how they will handle each case

Property Redress Scheme
This is a service provided for property agents and professionals to handle complaints made by a consumer i.e. a tenant. They will help the agent or professional to reach a solution with the tenant. The redress scheme is aimed at agents and landlords who have entered a rent to rent or guaranteed rent arrangement.

Data Protection Act

As you will be handling the personal information of tenants when referencing them and writing tenancy agreements you should be ethical with how you handle this information. To give tenants peace of mind you should register with the Information Commissioner's Office.

You have an obligation to handle personal data responsibly and maintain the security of the information. There are estate agents and property professionals who will pass on your data to third parties, this is not good practice.

Property litigation services

There are some lawyers that specialise in property and help you deal with any disputes with landlords, agents, and tenants. You should think about adding a specialist in this area to your team.

What sort of property is desired for Rent to Rent to work?

Ideally, a property that can market at least four rooms should be sought after; anything less and the property will not generate enough revenue to make a profit after the landlord's rent and utility bills have been paid. The property is likely to be detached, semi-detached or a three-storey terrace that is big enough to contain multiple bedrooms.

Sometimes a property may only be three or four bedroomed but has a downstairs reception room that can be converted into an extra rental room. As explained earlier HMO properties and single occupancy homes that are large enough will suit the Rent to Rent system. HMO properties will be more regulated and you will be under the scrutiny of the local council.

Single occupancy homes that have enough rooms may be small enough to avoid the regulations. You could go offer your service to these homes instead of HMOs but the market in the area may be limited and the properties are more likely to have a buy to let mortgage in place. The risk of a buy to let mortgage will be explained later.

Tenant demand

A tried and trusted method for testing the demand for your rooms in an area is through using dummy adverts. By using sites like Spareroom you can post an advert for a room to see what kind of response you get. You test the advert for a year and see what the demand is like during different seasons. You can also change the prices of the rooms to see if there is any change in the demand.

I have included a video on my YouTube channel Dixon Property Deals about how to assess demand and supply for Rent to Rent property in your local towns. By looking for how many people want rooms in a town compared to how many rooms are available in that area, you will build up the information to make a decision. You will be able to make the decision of whether to source a property suitable for Rent to Rent in that town or look at another area.

What price should be charged for a room?

This will depend on the market you are advertising your room for and the quality of the room. In some areas, rooms can be rented out as little as £200 per calendar month whereas other properties may have rooms charged at £500 per calendar month. London would be a typical area of the country where rents are going to be higher.

A high-quality décor room with an en-suite marketed to a working professional is going to have a much higher rent than a basic room occupied by a student. Once a decision has been made on whom to market and furnish the room too you can use property portals like Rightmove and Zoopla as well as Spareroom and similar sites to check the rent charged for similar accommodation in the area.

What kind of 'light refurbishment' is required for the property?

Each room may need walls redecorating and new carpets laid along with furnishings for the desired let. A student may require a desk, bed and a wardrobe for example. Utilities may need to be installed such as TV and internet broadband. Security is also a big issue with locks to be fitted on the doors of each room, so each tenant has a key to access the room.

Hiring professionals such as painter and decorators, carpet fitters, locksmiths, and joiners will be a requirement to get the property ready for letting. This will be the only significant cost to the Rent 2 Rent professional.

Renovating HMO property for Rent to Rent

Are you in the business of Rent 2 Rent or do you want to be property developer? If you want to be a property developer then Rent 2 Rent is not for you. Stay away from properties that need a full refurbishment and major structural work. If you take on this kind of property then you are going to have some substantial upfront costs on a property that, legally, you don't own. You are focusing on properties that need a light refurbishment where only a few thousand pounds is required to get the property in shape for letting rooms.

Viewings

At this point, you probably want to go over the figures and make sure that the property will be a viable business venture. You don't want to rush in and make an offer to a landlord or agent. This is a business and making quick decisions without thinking is not business like. You should follow this list of due diligence before and when viewing the property.

- Find out what the council tax will be on the property
- What are the local HMO regulations and planning permissions?
- How many bedrooms are in the property? Is there the possibility of converting more?

- Use Zoopla to check historical listings of the property to check previous prices and changes in floor plans
- Assess rental prices for similar rooms in the advertised in the local area. Again sites like Zoopla can assist you with this or talk to local letting agents.
- Does each bedroom have adequate safety exits in case of a fire?
- What is the overall standard of the house? Is there mould and damp?
- Does the property require refurbishment? E.g. new carpets, painting and decorating
- Is the owner/landlord managing it locally?
- Will there be any furnishings included?
- Are there any white goods included?
- What utility providers are there? Internet providers being a good example

For some of this information, you will be able to check before you visit the property for a viewing. It is handy when you go on your viewing to take a checklist for you to fill out as you go around the property. You can make notes on things that need sorting out before you can let a room out to tenants.

Running the numbers

Let's say that you have found the right property that you are looking for. You have done all your research and decided on the business model of HMO property. You have done local research and used tools on Zoopla and Rightmove to decide on charging £400 per calendar month for each room. The property you have found has six bedrooms and is in a great location just outside the city centre with great transport links and plenty of amenities.

The area is renowned for housing working professionals who have jobs in the city. Now you need to see what sort of yield you can achieve and what you are prepared to pay the landlord or agent as a monthly fee to control the property. A good aim for cash flow is £500 plus as a goal for your income from the property.

Yield

All six rooms rented @ £400 = £2,400 per month x 12 = £28,800 annually

Net gain

Income per month
    £2,400

Minus monthly costs
    £600
        Includes management
            advertising
            maintenance

Your monthly income goal
    £500

The maximum you are prepared
    £1,300
to pay the landlord or agent per month

The last figure can be negotiated with the landlord or agent and if you can get the monthly fee lower than the maximum then you can achieve more income than £500 per month.

This income figure of £500 doesn't seem like much but times by 12 months and you generate an income of £6,000 over the year. Once you are comfortable with managing one property you can start to expand and control more properties. Eventually, you can build the sort of salary that an executive manager would expect.

Making an offer

If you are organised and have handed over all your marketing materials that outline what you can offer as a rent to rent manager then you should be in a good position to make an offer. Always answer any questions that a potential landlord or agent may have.

You should also have copies of your rent to rent contracts to control and manage the property. It is very likely that they will want to read the legal terms of the contract and highlight anything they don't understand or are not comfortable with. It is your job to ease their mind that they are dealing with someone professional and that they can trust you during the period of the contract.

Once you have had several talks with the landlord or agent and if there seems to be positive feedback it is time to make an offer. This should be in writing and either sent by email or in the post. The offer should include details on what your management includes and the monthly fee you will pay. If there is an agreement for you to take control of the property then it is time for signatures on the rent 2 rent contract.

Marketing and advertising rooms

Marketing and advertising can be done by an online agent such as Upad or yourself. Online agents will charge a fee to advertise the room on major property portals but may also offer the service of vetting prospective tenants.

If advertised by yourself you may look at using sites like Gumtree, Spareroom, and Craigslist to advertise a room. The vetting and screening of tenants will also be done by you. This can be quite daunting to an inexperienced person. You will have to check references and read credit reports from agencies such as Experian and Equifax. It is better to pay a bit of money for peace of mind if this is an area you are not confident with, otherwise, you may be landed with rogue tenants who do not pay rent and neglect the room.

If marketing the rooms to low-income tenants or those on benefits it is important that immigration checks are carried out. Housing illegal immigrants are the last thing that you need.

The advertisement should clearly state the features of the room in terms of furnishings and utilities along with kitchen, bathroom and toilet facilities. It is a good idea to state what kind of tenant you are looking for such as a working professional or student.

You want to group similar types of a tenant as they are more likely to get on and share common interests. Include any rules in the description such as whether smoking and pets are allowed.

Managing tenants

Unlike a traditional buy-to-let or HMO where tenants are on an assured short-hold tenancy, tenants in a multi-let property will be issued a license for the room. This is a similar agreement to a lodger and has a very important aspect. The license will grant the landlord or in this case the rent 2 rent proprietor, access to the flat at any time.

An assured short-hold tenancy would mean the landlord having to contact the tenant for permission to access the property. They also would have to give 24 hours' notice before being able to enter. The license is important, especially if dealing with a lower class of tenant where problems may arise. There may be neglect to a room or disputes between tenants, so it is important that there is immediate access to sort the situation out.

At times you will need a thick skin and have to stand your ground, especially when evicting tenants. Firm but fair is the stance to be taken when managing problem tenants. Regular visits to properties are a must to check on tenants' behaviour and the standard of the rooms. I have a detailed eBook on managing HMO property which I have listed in the Education section of this guide.

Insurance

Contents Insurance
The rent to rent professional will need contents insurance to cover furniture that is provided in each room for tenants. This should cover any damage caused by the tenants and fires.

Professional Indemnity Insurance
You only need to take a policy if you feel you are giving a landlord or a tenant advice as part of your service. It may be wise to get professional indemnity insurance just in case a landlord or tenant is in a dispute over something they claim was from your advice.

Public Liability Insurance
This insurance is a must as someone such as a tenant may trip over something in the property which causes an injury. The person may then choose to sue your business for damages. Landlords will have their own liability insurance usually covered by their buildings insurance policy.

Employee Insurance

This is compulsory if you intend to employ staff on contracts with the business.

Owners Insurance Contributions
The landlord of the property will have the policy to cover the building. The policy will cover any damage to the structure or exterior of the property.

Are there any risks?

Most of the risk will fall with the landlord should the property be on a buy to let mortgage. Mortgage lenders can view the multi-let as a breach of the terms and conditions of the mortgage where the property should have a single let tenancy. There is also the risk of breaching a contract for landlord insurance on a buy to let property.

Although both are mainly a risk to the landlord they also have consequences for the Rent 2 Rent business as the expenditure on the refurbishment of the property may be lost. It is good practice to state this risk to prospective landlords so that both parties know what might happen before agreeing on a contract.

The other potential risk is that the landlord is not who he or she says they are. There is a lot of scam artists posing as landlords of properties they don't even own. Checking proof of identity, address and ownership is a must before agreeing to any contract agreement on a property.

Should a property be poorly managed then you risk the local authorities investigating the property. This could arise from neighbourhood complaints about noisy tenants and anti-social behaviour. The multi-let property could be closed down with authorities demanding it reverts back to single occupancy.

Look professional

It is important that your business looks professional so that prospective landlords and letting agents get a good impression. You need to build their trust that they can turn to your service.

Professional email

You cannot use a personal email account such as Gmail or Hotmail as you simply won't look professional. To look credible with landlords and agents you will need to purchase a professional email address. Email addresses are cheap and they can also be bought with a domain and a website.

Online presence

Should you be on a tight budget then utilising online networking sites like Linkedin and Facebook will be adequate to establish an online presence. You can use these networking sites to establish a page for your business where you can advertise your service and rooms to tenants.

A website can be built in the future but bear in mind that it will cost money to build and there will be on-going expenses to keep it running. Wordpress is a popular content system used to build simple websites and there are many others on the market. Which one you choose will be based on the cost to build and how easy it is for you to use.

Business cards

You are going to need these to leave with a landlord or agent, so they can contact you in the future should they need your service. They could be crucial in winning some future business because a landlord or agent may not be interested at first but may change their mind months later. If they still have your card they will get in touch.

The card should have the business name and logo, your name and title, the business address, phone and email details and a website address should you have one.

Call-answering service

This will help the business look professional by having a call-answering service set up. The business can also feel more corporate and build credibility. The service will also be useful when you are out and about traveling to properties or visiting agents. You will know that your business will never miss calls and therefore miss out on potential leads. By having initial calls answered by the online receptionist you can also give yourself a bit of time to deal with the enquiry rather than dealing with it there and then from the first call. This will help you if you're the nervous type on the phone.

Chapter Ten: Lease options trading

Perhaps you are an investor who has become frustrated by the difficulties of raising more finance to build your portfolio. Or maybe you are just deciding on whether to invest in property but lack the capital or the access to finance to buy your first investment property.

Since the credit crunch of 2008, lending criteria to make investments in buy to let, HMO property and developments have become increasingly strict. You've got to have significant deposits to achieve good deals and have a very good level of income in order to qualify for a loan. For most, property investment is only a dream that really can never be achieved.

But what if I told you that there is another way. You can choose another way of building a portfolio of property; no need to go through the traditional channels to raise finance. There is a relatively new strategy out there being used by property investors right now to acquire residential property; a form of contract that has been used for many years in the commercial property world. This contract agreement is known as a lease option.

What are lease options?

There is a long history of how options became an investment strategy and they were not initially used to invest in property. Hundreds of years ago options were used to buy corn, meat, and other agricultural produce in order to safeguard against market changes. Buyers would use options to lock in the product at a certain price. The buyer would acquire goods at a price that would not be too affected by a downturn in the market. In the past century, lease options have become a popular way to invest in residential and commercial property, especially in the United States. Lease options are still yet to take off in the United Kingdom and therefore present an excellent opportunity for an entrepreneur to enter the property market. Below is probably the best definition of what a lease option is:

'An option agreement is a legal document that gives the holder the option to buy or not to buy a property. The seller must sell the property to the holder if he or she takes up the option.'

The seller is bound by law to sell the property to the option holder but the holder does not have to buy it. Sometimes the option can grant the permission to the holder to live in the home or find a tenant as well as having the legal right to buy the property within a time period. We will go over the different ways lease options can be used in this guide.

Options are a great way to invest in property providing choice and control over a property. The most successful property developers, like Donald Trump, have used property options to generate incredible wealth. Options provide the opportunity for an investor to make substantial cash flow without ownership of bricks and mortar asset. You don't need to get permission from anyone else but the seller. No dealing with banks, lenders, mortgage brokers, credit referencing, large deposits and solicitors.

Regulation of lease options
As the market for lease options is still not that popular in the UK there is currently no recognised regulation for this kind of contract. However, it is wise that your

business engages with property sellers in a professional manner and act as if your business was regulated.

The Financial Services Authority is monitoring the way lease options are being used and may well release legislation in the future. They are looking to put more pressure on property dealers and lease options investors due to lease options being viewed as a grey area along with mortgage fraud and no money down investment.

How to make lease options work

You are going to need certain things to be in your favour for the deal to work. You need to know what is needed to make the lease option a legally binding and enforceable contract between you, the option holder, and the seller. You have to know what is needed for you to be able to control the property without legal ownership. Below is a list of what you need for an option agreement:

- A seller who is willing and motivated
- Property or land that is the asset to be controlled
- A written agreement with granted privileges
- An option or consideration fee
- The agreed purchase price
- An agreed time period
- A buyer

Without all of these parts, you don't have what you need to complete a lease option agreement.

Motivated seller

The seller needs to understand the terms of the lease option and be comfortable with the agreement. There should be no deception or coercion into the option agreement. Many sellers will ask why they should agree to this and it is your job to convince them that this is right for them. This should be done with honesty and integrity that clearly defines the outcomes of the agreement so that both parties are happy.

An asset

There needs to be something attractive or desirable that has value for the option to work effectively. This could be a property or land. You need to ensure that the asset has real value. You don't want to invest in a property that is due for demolition. With an option agreement of just £1, this outcome would be bearable. However, if you had invested thousands of pounds with a more traditional investment you are not going to be happy about it. This is one of the attractive things about lease options; the risk is far less than with other investment strategies.

A written agreement

Options require a written agreement as they are all about terms, permissions and conditions. A verbal agreement can lead to disputes where either party could veer off the original agreement. The seller could backtrack on the agreement to sell at an agreed price. You as the holder may not pay the agreed monthly rent on a property or you may get in a tenant without permission. For fairness to both parties, it is important to have the original agreement in writing. You can always agree to make changes to the contract at a later date. The agreement should also have a time period before the agreement becomes void.

The fee

An option fee, or consideration fee, make the written agreement legally binding, like a deed. You should think of it as the signature for the agreement. The amazing thing is that in the UK there is no minimum value for the option agreement to become valid. Most options dealers will typically use a value of just £1 for the agreement. It is important to recognise that £1 does not buy you the house! It simply gives you the control of the property.

Purchase price

You want your standard offer on the purchase of the property based on a reducing amount rather than a fixed price offer. However, the payment amount should be clear to the seller whichever way you structure. Let's say you are interested in purchasing a house worth £200,000 that has a mortgage of £160,000 secured. Now we will analyse three scenarios of structuring the payment of the purchase price over a five-year period.

1. A fixed purchase price of £185,000
2. A purchase price of £210,000 minus your monthly payments of £600
3. A purchase price at the redemption amount (to clear the loan) plus £3,000

Two of these purchase prices do not specify an actual amount but rather an amount that is dependent on when the property is bought i.e. the five-year period.

Now see what you pay for each of the payment structures.

1. The purchase price will be £185,000 in the sixtieth month, no change
2. The second structure would result in a payment of £174,000 in the sixtieth month
3. The third choice where the loan will reduce by £300 per month would mean you paying £145,000 in month sixty

Obviously, the third choice of payment structure will result in the best price for you. Although, this doesn't mean you are going to get that kind of deal. Through negotiation, you will know what the seller is after and that third choice may not be attractive.

But there will be some sellers that will be in a bad situation that requires a solution to clear the debt quickly. In this case, the third choice will be a very effective method of getting the property at a heavily discounted price and clearing the debts of the seller. It all depends on the mindset of the person selling the property; some people can't handle having a big debt hanging over them.

Timeframe
We've just seen how important the time frame can be to structuring a deal and getting a decent purchase price for the property. By law, you can only issue an option agreement for up to 21 years in the United Kingdom. So don't structure any deals for any longer period, otherwise the option agreement can be thrown out of court should the seller challenge the original purchase price agreed.

Line up a buyer

For you to make income from this deal you need to find a buyer. This could be a buyer who has already made a pre-agreement to purchase the property at a price. Or, it may be a tenant-buyer who will move into the property, take care of it, pay a monthly rent and buy the property at the end of the time frame. The buyer must understand the terms of the agreement or the privilege to buy the property at an agreed price will be lost.

Purchase options

Purchase options are considered to be the most straightforward agreements in the property options group. An agreement can be written on one page. The option grants you the exclusive right to buy the property within a time frame. They are a great way to make money from being a middleman or to secure a discounted property. You could use a purchase option to:

- Secure a property at a discounted price and lock out other potential buyers until the purchase is completed
- Secure the right to buy an empty property that requires improvement and modernising; improve and add value and then sell the option
- Improve the property under the option to increase the value, you can then choose to buy the property or sell the option
- Use an option to secure the right to buy a property at the present market value then obtain planning permission and sell the option on to a property developer

An example of how a purchase option could work:

An owner has a residential property that has a large enough garden for another house to be built upon. The market value for the property is £250,000 and the owner has agreed to sell at this price. The investor takes up the option to purchase the property within a 12 month period at a fee of £200.

The investor then obtains planning permission for a new house and the price for the current property rises to £300,000. The option holder would then have two choices with what to do with the property. Sell the purchase option with the planning permission in place. The property is now worth £300,000 and the option is worth £50,000. The option can be sold for a fee.

Another choice for the investor is to divide the land and keep existing property but sell the land with the planning permission as a plot to build on.

Sandwich options

This is an effective investment strategy involving lease options but does involve risk. This is where you, as the holder of the option, have the option to buy the seller's property but grant someone else, another investor (wealthy and cash rich), the ownership of the option to buy the property.

This is an excellent strategy for investors who have low capital. The original option holder will have to establish an agreement with the property owner and then find a lessee of their own who will buy the option. The property may require a bit of equity by the original option holder (i.e. you) to keep the property well maintained and managed until a buyer is found.

This option agreement does create a bit of risk to the original option holder if he or she spends a large amount to maintain the property but can't find a buyer during the option agreement period. The option holder makes a profit on the sale of the option by taking a fee (the cost of the option) from the wealthy investor.

Cooperative options

This kind of options deal will give the tenant-buyer greater security than a sandwich option but will provide three areas of income from the deal for the investor. The points of income will be at the time the end buyer moves in, monthly income during the term and when the tenant-buyer exercises the option to buy. You will need to look for the right property and the right seller for a cooperative option to work.

The properties ideally suited to cooperative options are family homes in desirable locations. The property will be ready to let and have the potential for capital growth. The property will need to achieve good monthly credits to the purchase price providing attractive terms to the tenant-buyer and profits that can be shared with all parties.

The seller needs to be in a strong position where there have been no missed payments and no arrears on mortgage repayments. The seller will need to be willing to let the property until a sale is completed. The seller will need to be comfortable with letting the investor (option holder) manage the tenancy until the sale completion.

The investor will collect a fee upon the agreement for the tenant-buyer to move in and the Option Agreement is assigned over. The monthly rent will be paid to the investor as part of the management agreement who will be able to keep a percentage of this with the rest being paid to the seller.

When the tenant buyer exercises the option to buy then the share of profits is allocated to the seller and the investor according to the agreement. Should the tenant-buyer decide not to exercise the option agreement then the contract reverts to the investor again.

What skills will you need?

There are a number of key skills that you are going to need to make lease options a successful investment strategy. Each individual seller or buyer is going to have different needs and requirements.

You are going to have to listen to what they are saying so that you can gauge what would be the right agreement for a successful deal. By listening to what a person is saying and getting a grasp of the meaning behind the words you can be flexible in your negotiation. People are not going to agree to a contract if you don't show interest in their situation. Make sure you pay attention to what they are saying and that you hear everything.

The more complicated a lease option is the more likely there is going to be disagreements and disputes that could lead to legal action. By keeping lease options simple between yourself, the seller and the end buyer you prevent a negative outcome from happening.

When speaking to all parties about the terms of the agreement, make sure they fully understand everything. Your sellers and buyers should have all the relevant information in writing that you should be able to explain easily without getting into a muddle yourself.

You should be comfortable in dealing with people from all walks of life, which is part of the reason why each individual will have different needs and wants from a deal. You are going to be dealing with investors, developers, landlords, other dealers, tenants, and homeowners. This is a very people-intensive occupation. You are going to need good customer service skills so it will help if you have had previous customer service or sales experience.

You have to ask the question, "Why would anyone choose to do a deal with me?" Are you trustworthy with good intentions and act with integrity? Do you have a seller's or buyer's priorities in mind? Can you get on easily with people and be easy to work with? If your answer is no to all or some of these questions then using lease options is not a good fit for you.

However, you can develop these skills and with practice and experience, you will become a professional lease option investor.

How to find motivated sellers

Sellers become motivated to sell by their emotions not because they are thinking logically. They have ownership of a property that they no longer want and they feel trapped. The situation has become a drain and they are desperate to get out.

Each seller will have different circumstances from the other. One seller may have just experienced a divorce. Another seller may have inherited an empty property and would rather have the cash. Perhaps the seller just doesn't like where they live anymore. Whatever the reason they will be experiencing negative emotions and are more likely to be interested in your potential solution.

You want the seller to be able to move on and be free and enjoy life again. Couples that experience a break-up and those that are in financial difficulties are the two best cases where a lease option will work.

Lease options in cases of separated and divorced couples

Couples that have had a relationship breakdown and have separated or divorced will want out as soon as possible. They will no longer want to be tied to the property, either financially or emotionally. The property just brings back painful memories. It is likely the couple has taken out a mortgage on the property.

You can structure a deal using a lease option so that all parties can be released from the property. The deal could involve a payment made to the couple (separate to each party) and by using a lengthy lease option you can avoid hefty early repayment charges on a mortgage. Most mortgage lenders will charge a fee if the property is sold within a few years from the date the mortgage was taken. By waiting to buy the property after this period you avoid triggering this repayment charge which will save the couple money.

Lease options in cases where there are owners in financial difficulty

Sellers may run into difficulties paying a mortgage on a property due to changes in their circumstances. By offering a long-term lease option and installing a tenant-buyer you can cover the mortgage payments whilst be making some profit margin. The seller can move into a more affordable property. They no longer have to worry about the property or have the hassle of having to find and manage tenants.

Eventually, the option to buy is taken and the property is no longer a burden.

How to market to motivated sellers

Those have had experience in property dealing or investing in property in the local area will have an advantage. You should be targeting properties that are at mid-to-high value rather than low-value properties that might be more suitable for below market value trading.

By getting to know these areas you can target your campaign to this demographic. Focus on three avenues of marketing, social media in conjunction with a landing page, newspaper adverts, leaflet drops and listings sites.

Social media like Facebook, YouTube and Instagram would be a great start for advertising to sellers. You can put posts on Facebook and Instagram and pay for the posts to be marketed to a certain demographic. You will need to advertise your landing page for sellers to fill in contact information and details about their property. This is known as a lead which you can then use to contact the seller by phone and discuss how you can help.

YouTube will be a little bit different because you will be using videos to market to sellers in your area. Your videos only need to be two minutes or less with details about what you can offer and the area you do business. Again you need to include the web address for your landing page.

You can get your landing page designed by a professional on freelancing sites like Fiverr or Upwork for a very low price. You could do it yourself with websites like Ontrapages that enable you to design your own landing pages.

Your local newspaper is a great channel for you to use to advertise your business to local homeowners. You need to emphasize in the advert that you are able to help distressed owners. The advert only needs to be in the lower-priced classified section for the property. Newspaper adverts will probably be the most costly marketing channel for you to use. Adverts could cost you up to £50 to run for two weeks.

You can do leaflet drops in local areas with the desired property you are looking for. You are looking for the more upmarket housing estates on your map. Your leaflets only need to be an A5 size and black and white will do. What is important is that your leaflet has the right information about what you can do and your contact details. You should also make sure that you keep sending leaflets in the same area periodically. People are not going pick up the phone if you just send one leaflet. It can be after many leaflets have been sent to a household before they might contact you. You have to get known in your area and building awareness can take time.

You have to convince homeowners to use your service rather than traditional routes like using an estate agent. A truly motivated seller will be interested when they are in a desperate situation that they want to get out of. You might want to think about posting letters, rather than leaflets, to empty properties to try to establish contact with the vendor.

You can use listing sites like Gumtree and Craigslist to post adverts for your local area. You should make regular weekly posts with details of what you can do along with contact details or your landing page. Make the adverts enticing with a good title like 'sell your house fast' along with the town or city that you are targeting. Include details about how you can help distressed sellers and tired landlords.

You can also contact landlords, agents and homeowners who have listed adverts in newspapers, on listings sites and online through property portals like Zoopla and Rightmove. By using the tools on property portals and having regular contact with local estate agents you can filter your search to narrow down to the properties that have been on the market a while. This is going to lead you to motivated sellers that may have problems in selling their property. By doing a bit of investigation you can find out why the property is not selling and think about a solution using lease options. Sometimes it might involve calling vendors with property for sale or those that have property to rent. Either way, it can lead to a successful property deal.

You should let all advertising sit for a while, typically two or three weeks, before contacting a seller. This will help with filtering motivated sellers. When making the call to a seller, you should ask if the property is still on the market. If the seller has found a buyer then you can move on but if not then you know that you have a motivated seller.

Calling a vendor with a house for sale

Below is a typical conversation that you should have with a vendor who has a property for sale. The aim is to establish whether there is an opportunity to use a lease option agreement with the vendor. A purchase option or sandwich option would be suitable in this scenario. Your first question should be:

"Hello, my name is Joe Bloggs and I've just come across your property for sale on Zoopla. Is the property still for sale?"

If the answer is yes then ask a few questions and listen to what the vendor is saying about the property. You might be able to find out whether the vendor has found it difficult to sell the property. Listen out for how they talk if they seem unenthusiastic it may be that they are fed up with the property and want the burden off their hands.

Or it may be that they are desperate to sell (property needs a repair, little equity, and a large mortgage, the financial situation has changed). Try to be positive and build a rapport explaining a little about how you can help. Your follow up question should be:

"Okay, I think I can help you with your situation… I am looking for a property to buy within the next (time period for the lease option e.g. five years)…"

If the vendor of the property does not seem keen on the idea then move on but leave them your contact details in case they change their mind.

Calling a vendor with a house for rent

Below is a typical conversation that you should have with a vendor who has a property to rent. Remember, you are trying to establish whether there is the opportunity to use a lease option – either a sandwich option or cooperative option. Your first question should be:

"Hello, my name is Joe Bloggs and I've just seen your ad on Gumtree. Is the property still available to rent?"

If the answer is yes then ask a few questions and listen to what the vendor is saying about the house. Try to establish rapport and build a positive vibe which will help when viewing the property. You should follow up on the questions with the next question:

"That's great….I'm looking for a property that I can rent long term with the option to buy…"

Avoid wasting time with property vendors who will never sell. Use this script and if the vendor is not positive and is only interested in a tenant then move on.

Sourcing property from an estate agent

By doing research from your home you can utilise a completely free way to source property that would be suitable for a lease option agreement. You can view the websites of estate agents in your local area or use property portals.

When reading the adverts for property for sale you should look out for words like 'available'. Also look at the photos of the property and ask yourself 'does the property look empty?" You can start to do your research on the property before viewing to decide on what needs to be done to the property to get it ready for sale or to let. You can also gauge the financial situation of the seller.

You must avoid repossessed property as they are not suitable for a lease option agreement so make sure you find this information out, either from the estate agent. Some properties advertised may only have an external shot so this might be a clue that it is repossession. Sometimes the estate agent might be a bit cagey about revealing repossessed properties so you might have to listen to what they are saying to get clues that it is repossession or get the vendor's contact details (you may have to get the vendor's information from the land registry). This approach is a very cheap and effective method of hunting for properties.

Taking a look at the property

When you view this property use this time to start negotiating with the seller and begin thinking about a deal that will achieve a win-win situation. Firstly, you need to connect with the seller by building rapport. Show an interest in them and their lives and make nice comments on their property as you do the viewing. You need to put them at ease with yourself so that they feel comfortable talking to you.

Find a place to sit and discuss what you can do for the seller; ideally, you should be aiming for an agreement. If you can't reach an agreement ask them kindly that you cannot help and would like to leave. Make sure they have your contact details if they were to change their mind on an agreement. You really need to get a grasp of the emotion that the seller is going through and try to bring this out in the conversation. You will find out how desperate they are to get out of the situation. This can also help you to avoid any remorse you may feel for buying the property from a distressed seller.

Many view lease options as bad ethically but at the end of the day, you are there to offer an agreement that will help them to get out of a bad situation. Discuss the choices the seller has and be prepared that an option agreement may not be the best choice. The seller will have the choice of an option agreement, to sell, to let or to wait.

Discuss deadlines for the offer an option agreement and persuade them that by giving you the permission to rent now and buy later will be doing something to help right away. Make sure you verify all of the seller's information in terms of the asking price, the mortgage, unsecured debt and the monthly payments. Once you have an option agreement the property could become your liability, so it is very important that you verify the information.

Only make the offer of an option agreement when you know you have a structured deal that will work. Let the idea play around in the seller's head and don't push it. Give them a bit of time to make the decision.

Dealing with objections

Never get despondent when you hear objections from the owner of the property. You should perceive these objections as selling signals that can actually present an opportunity. By dealing with these objections effectively you can help the seller make the right decision for their property.

When the owner objects to any part of the lease option agreement you put forward listen carefully to what they are actually saying. Put the question back to them why they think it is too low and try clarifying if it is just a test or if there is a genuine objection. Carefully explain your lease option offer and go over the details to make sure the seller fully understands it.

Rent to buy

Rent to buy is also known by other names such as rent to own and lease to own. Rent to buy can be set up neatly by using a cooperative option bringing two parties, motivated sellers and tenant-buyers, together into the deal. The rent to buy scheme gives the buyer (the tenant-buyer) a legal right to purchase the property at an agreed price within a time frame.

The tenant-buyer has to make monthly payments in order to keep this legal right. The tenant-buyer will also have to keep the property well maintained during the tenancy as if the property were their own. A tenant-buyer will be willing to pay more for a property for the following reasons:

- The purchase price is fixed during the term and won't change
- The tenant-buyer does not have to purchase the property and can walk away once the term has finished
- The tenant-buyer can treat the property as their own home
- The tenant-buyer can move in quickly without waiting for legal paperwork to go through like a traditional sale of a property
- The tenant-buyer can make improvements on the property
- The tenant-buyer has the opportunity to 'try before you buy'
- The tenant-buyer can exercise the option to buy when they decide
- The tenant-buyer can either build up a deposit or have some of the rent credited to the balance of the purchase

As the option holder, the investor will benefit from a rent to buy scheme under a cooperative option.

- No requirement for a mortgage or deposit
- Less management required as the tenant-buyer will take care of the property
- Collect a sum at the start of the deal
- Receive a monthly income from the rent after paying the monthly fee to the landlord
- Profit on the sale of the property when the tenant-buyer exercises the option to buy

The landlord, or vendor, will also have a number of benefits from a rent to buy scheme:

- The tenant-buyers will have a homeowner mindset and will take care of the property rather than a typical renter who may neglect the property
- The vendor can sell a house that may be stuck on the market
- Higher rents will be paid as the tenant will be willing to pay more to secure the property
- The vendor can collect a lump sum when the tenant moves in
- Fewer calls from tenant buyers complaining about maintenance issues e.g. boiler broken down, bulbs need replacing
- Less likely to have tenants who will fall into arrears on the rent as tenant buyer's right to buy will depend on payments being made

From the lists above you can see that all parties involved in the deal are set to gain something. Lease options should be used to create a win-win situation not just to make money for you.

Avoiding problems

In this section, I have included some tips based on my experiences in property dealing. Through mistakes, I have learnt how to become more effective at lease option agreements and I am sharing my advice with you.

Don't be too keen

When starting out it is easy to get carried away. You are chomping at the bit and can't wait to make deals and seeing the pound signs lighting up in front of you. By rushing into a deal when I started out it cost me £6000. This was because I was too keen to do any deal and rushed in without taking my time and doing my due diligence.

If there are any doubts about the deal go through the information and ask the seller or the buyer more questions. You want to get the right answers before committing and signing to an agreement.

Due Diligence

I have already just mentioned due diligence but it is very important in today's world where identity theft and fraud is common. This is what cost me my £6000 because I didn't check that the vendor actually owned the property legally. When analysing a deal, make sure all parties are whom they say they are.

Make sure the seller has their name on the deeds and vet your potential tenant-buyer to ensure they will make monthly payments. Your tenant-buyer may have a bad history of missing payments and has a poor credit rating. It is your duty to yourself and the seller that you manage the tenancy professionally so you don't want to install bad tenants.

There are many lease option investors who will offer a property to tenants with poor credit history and I believe this is bad practice. By putting in a potentially bad tenant then you put the whole deal at risk and could put you, as the lease option holder, in legal and financial trouble.

Contingency Plan

A wise move would be to build a contingency fund so that you have cash available should a tenant-buyer default on a monthly payment. Your agreement with the seller will be to make a monthly payment even if you do not receive payment from your tenant.

A good strategy is to keep putting aside some of the cash you receive from the tenant-buyer and your fund will build quickly. Although missed payments are stressful enough it won't feel as bad should you have no money to pay the vendor!

Use Professional Contracts

You should make sure that your contracts are professional. Ignore the temptation to download and use a template from the internet. Instead, pay for an experienced solicitor to draw one up for you. Use a solicitor who has had experience with property professionals who have used lease option contracts.

By networking with local business people and property professionals you will find a qualified professional who will assist you for a fee. It is better spending a little bit here rather than running into problems with sellers and tenant-buyers that could lead to costly legal fees.

Chapter Eleven: Buying repossessed property

What is the meaning of 'repossession'?
'Repossession' of a property involves the lender taking back the property from the borrower. This usually happens when there is a default such as a failure to meet payments. When a borrower takes out a mortgage, the property will be used as security against the loan. The borrower will sign a 'mortgage deed' that should say that if he or she does not keep up with the repayments the property will be repossessed.

What happens once a property is repossessed?
A property will be placed on the market for sale either by an estate agent or through auction. The proceeds from the sale will go to the lender. If the amount made from the sale does not cover the amount borrowed then the borrower is liable for the remaining balance. This includes any costs for the possession order. Other costs can be added to the balance including arrears, insurance, legal fees and lender's fees. The lender has 12 years to recover the debt via the courts, starting from the date the borrower first fell into arrears.

How does a lender obtain possession?
Lenders will repossess property only as a last resort when payment plans have failed. This is usually when the borrower has fallen into arrears over two to six months. The lender can repossess a property in three ways:

Voluntary Agreement
A borrower will agree to hand over the keys to the property to the lender after deciding that they cannot

continue to pay the mortgage. The lender will ask the borrower to sign a document called a 'voluntary possession declaration' as confirmation of agreement to the decision and that there is still liability for all mortgage payments and costs until the sale of the property. This is the most amicable agreement and can result in a quick sale.

Surrender or abandon the property
If the borrower falls into arrears and is unwilling to discuss financial problems with the lender, the keys may be handed over to the lender without discussion ('surrender') or move out of the property without notifying the lender ('abandon').

In the case of abandonment the terms of the mortgage will have been breached if two payments have been missed, notice for payment is ignored or a further three months of payments are missed and the borrower cannot be contacted at the mortgaged address.

Court Order
If outstanding arrears cannot be recovered by the lender and if the property has not been abandoned or surrendered, then a decision will be made to go to court to obtain a possession order. The lender will have to comply with all legal procedures when initiating court proceedings.

The repossession process

There are seven stages in the repossession process that must be followed legally by a lender. The owner can seek legal advice to stop the repossession of the property.

The process will begin with a written letter from the lender asking for arrears to be paid. If the lender is not happy with the response from the owner or there is no response another letter will be sent warning that court action will start to repossess the home.

The next stage will be the lender applying to court for a 'possession order'. Without this the lender cannot legally repossess the property.

The court will then send a letter to the owner issuing claim form and a date for the court hearing. The hearing is where the judge will decide whether the property will be repossessed by the lender or that the owner can keep the house. The claim form will also include a defence form for the owner to complete. The owner will usually use an adviser or solicitor to help prepare for the hearing and show evidence.

The judge will make a decision at the hearing. The decision could be repossession and the owner can be evicted, or suspended possession order where the owner has to agree to repay arrears in instalments, or adjourn the case to a later date or dismiss the case against the owner.

If the property is to be repossessed the judge will decide on a date when the owner is to leave the property and a possession order is granted to the lender with this date on it. If it is a suspended order then the owner can live in the property as long as the instalments are met. The owner may also be ordered to pay the court costs.

If the owner has not moved out of the property by the date on the court order for possession, the lender can ask the courts bailiffs to remove the owner from the property. The lender must apply for a bailiff's warrant and the costs can also be charged to the owner. The bailiffs will write to the owner to confirm the date when they will visit the property.

When the owner is evicted and the property is repossessed the lender will take steps to sell the property. The owner will still be liable for payments of interest on the loan and capital repayments until the property is sold.

The ethical issues of buying repossessed property

There are ethical issues when it comes to deciding to buy a repossessed property and this comes down to your personal morals. A person or family will have been evicted and they now have to move in with other family, rent from a private landlord, find a home with a housing association or become homeless. The borrower will struggle to get another mortgage and if they do then there may be a charge on the new property and sales proceeds will go to paying the previous lender.

When someone buys a repossessed property they will often find personal items left behind. Some of these items can be very personal such as wedding photos and pictures of children. The estate agent who sold the property may be unwilling to inform you of the address of the evicted owner or be willing to forward the items. The agent may not even know the whereabouts of the previous occupier. You may have to dispose the items which may be upsetting to you or leave you with feelings of guilt.

Lenders are legally allowed to dispose any items left in the property before the sale. They have no obligation to forward personal items if the correct procedures have been followed. However, the lender is likely not to enter lofts and basements where items could have been stored. This means the clearance of the items lies with you and you have to be prepared to deal with this.

Where to find a repossessed property?

There are several ways of finding repossessed property; however it requires some investigation on your part. Advertisements for property very rarely state whether the property is repossessed. As a buyer you will need to know the marketing and advertising procedures by auctioneers and estate agents, how to spot a repossessed property and how to beat the competition.

Getting information from estate agents

An estate agent will more likely advertise a property as 'distressed sale' or 'property in distress' rather than as a repossessed property. Properties included under these terms include those where the owner has died or a repossession. Both offer the potential of buying the property below market value. A larger national chain of estate agents is more likely to sell a property on behalf of a lender such as a bank or building society. Many estate agents will be unwilling to disclose the specifics of a property particularly if you suspect that the property is repossessed. When visiting local estate agents it is best to just ask if they deal with repossessed properties. Many will say that they don't deal in these properties so you can then concentrate on the agents that do have repossessed properties on their books. Again estate agents may not disclose whether the property is repossessed but may state that it is a 'distressed sale'.

Getting information from auctioneers

When a property has been repossessed and it has been left in a poor state of repair it is more likely to be sold through an auction. Property investors and developers are more likely to be interested in this kind of property. An auction may be used if the lender has failed to sell the property through an estate agent. To find local auctions you should ask estate agents if they know of any auctions in the area. You should contact the auction house and sign up to their mailing list. The auction house will send catalogues of auctions that take place in your area.

Auctions are likely to use the term 'by order of mortgagee' rather than state that the listing is a repossessed property. Sometimes the auction house will be instructed not to advertise as a repossessed property in the catalogue by the lender but may advertise in local newspapers. The adverts may include clues such as the sellers address belonging to a bank or building society or the mention of a liquidator.

Reading the local newspapers

Lenders are under a duty to receive the best possible price for a repossessed property. If the selling agent has received an offer for the property, then it will be advertised for a period of seven days or more if it generates a lot of interest. The agent will use the local press and newspapers using the procedure 'notice of offer'. The advert will be placed in housing or small advert section of the publication.

By reading these adverts you will increase the chances of finding a repossessed property and may well be the first time you get an indication that a property is repossessed. The adverts will include details on the property including the current offer that has been made. The advert will encourage written offers above the current bid.

Online sources

You can register with online newspapers to search for previous adverts with 'notice of offer'. You can also get an idea of what properties sold at in the area. There are also specialist online sites for repossessed properties but beware sites that ask for payment fees to register.

A good site that I recommend is Repolist, which takes all of the trouble out of using property portals to search through hundreds of properties to find a possible repossession. Repolist have done this task for you, it is then down to you to do your due diligence and view the property to see if you have a deal. You do have to pay a monthly fee but it is one of the more reputable sites around.

Estate agents and auctioneers will have websites that will have forms for mailing lists that can keep you updated on properties that come on the market. This will be a good source of new property coming onto the market.

The statistics for repossessions in the UK

Since the recovery from the credit crunch and recession the number of repossessed houses in the UK has fallen. At the time of writing this book in February 2015 it was at its lowest in eight years. According to the Council of Mortgage Lenders (CML), the number of repossessions fell by 26% last year to 21,000 compared with 28,900 in 2013.

There were also fewer mortgages in arrears at the end of 2014 than at any time since 2006. Only 1.05% of all loans were in arrears of 2.5% or more on the mortgage balance compared with 1.29% at the end of 2013.Unemployment and interest rates are at low levels but the CML warns that the low interest rates will not last forever. Borrowers have to be careful when assessing the affordability of a mortgage not only in the present but in the future when interest rates will rise.

Research conducted by market research agency ICM published late 2014 suggests that a third of mortgage borrowers will struggle with repayments if interest rates rise by two percentage points.

Despite the likelihood that rates will start to upturn, only 14% of respondents as a whole – including mortgage holders, but also other non-borrowers – suggested to ICM that they had been making financial adjustments to deal with any rise.

Research

The property is not a bargain until you know it is being sold at the right price. You need to do a thorough price analysis so that you know when a bargain is placed on the market. You also need to think about the location.

Different locations will vary in prices and you will need to know your intended location well in order to spot a bargain.

Price analysis

You should regularly analyse changes in property prices both locally and nationally by visiting estate agents, monitoring the press and searching property websites.

The Halifax and Nationwide building societies both have their own house price indexes. Both sites have survey data on the housing market and you can get average prices for the region you live in. Both the sites have a house price calculator so that you can get an idea how your property has changed in price over a certain time period. The land registry also has a house price index based on sales data whether for cash or with a mortgage since 2000. The data can be searched nationally, by region or county with over details of over seven million sales.

The Council for Mortgage Lenders also provides up to date information and research that you can access from their website (www.cml.org.uk). There are useful reports and research on the performance of the housing market that can be downloaded.
Sites like Rightmove also have current value estimations and previous sales data.

Choosing your location

The more flexible you are on the location with which to buy your property the greater your chances are of buying a bargain property. The amount you can afford will have a major influence on what locations you are interested in. When you have conducted a thorough price analysis you will know what the average selling prices are in that location.

Other factors other than the price should be taken into account:

- What is the stability of the market? Are prices stable, falling or rising? Falling prices could leave you with negative equity in the property
- Are there environmental issues with the property such as flooding or pollution that could affect your finances or health?
- Are there any planned future developments that could affect the price of the property or make it hard to sell?
- If you have a family would they be happy living in the location? Is there good access to health services, shops, schools and entertainment?
- If the property were to be a buy to let then are there enough tenants in the area? Is there room for another buy to let landlord? What rent will you be able to charge? Is the return on investment good enough? Speak to local agents and landlord groups to network and gather information on who is operating in the area

Problem locations can cause the following issues and should be avoided:

- Areas of flooding could mean high premiums on the building insurance. You could lose possessions and become homeless if the area was to flood again
- A proposed highway scheme in the location could result in you having to sell your property and the land to the Secretary of State for Transport. If it is built nearby the property the noise and pollution could affect your quality of life. It will also make the property hard to sell and let

- A nearby airport will also make it hard to sell and let a property not to mention the stress of the noise if you live there
- Areas of degeneration are also a problem where there are empty and boarded up properties. The area will attract crime, vandals and squatters. The property is more likely to be damaged and broken into making Insurance premiums rise. The property will be difficult to attract purchasers and tenants.

Finding a bargain

Through conducting a thorough price analysis and carrying out location research you should be able to spot a property that is below market value when it appears on the market. You should regularly use sources to inform you when a property comes on the market so that you can act quickly. Look at locations that may regenerate near to more expensive areas. You could find a cheaper property that may rise in value quickly due to increasing popularity. Look out for increased investment in the area.

Choosing a property

You are now at the stage when you want to get out and about and view properties. As a prospective buyer it is important to keep records of your viewings. Recording features, maintenance and repair issues along with the price are important so that you have background research when it comes to looking at other properties.

Create the checklist

It is important to create a checklist that you can take with you when you view a property. The checklist can help you to discard properties that don't meet your criteria and concentrate on a well-suited property. Include on your checklist what is essential, what is desirable and features about which you are flexible. Features that might be essential are the location and the number of bedrooms. Features that you might find desirable are that the property has a rear garden and has got new windows and doors.

View the property
This is where you need to use your own senses to evaluate the condition of the property.

Use your sight to check for cracks in the walls, damp patches, stains or repaired concrete. Also look for signs of infestations, rot and decay.

Use your sense of smell to check for signs of damp, dry rot and wet rot. If there is a particular strong smell ask for an explanation from the selling agent. If the answer is inadequate then you will need to seek the advice from an expert.

Use your hearing to check for noises such as from nearby traffic, noisy neighbours or aeroplanes. Check for creaky floorboards that could indicate rot and decay. Ask the selling agent to demonstrate the boiler system if installed and check for any unusual sounds. Again ask for an explanation if anything unusual happens.

Use your sense of touch to feel for cracks and bumps in the plaster. Feel the woodwork around windows and under stairs if it is crumbling then this could indicate rot or infestation.

When viewing the property you should ask questions of the selling agent. Questions should include:

- How long has the property been empty?
- Why is the house for sale?
- How long has the property been tenanted (if relevant)?
- What is the type of ownership is on the property?
- Is the property a repossession?

You should ask as many questions as possible to get as much information on the property. You may view things and need clarification such as if there is a communal area or if there is an alteration to the building. If the property is a leasehold flat what are the ground rent and service charges?

Get expert advice

If you think there is anything wrong with the property whether it is stains, damp, cracking in brickwork, mould, alterations or other issues then get an expert opinion. Use a tradesman that is independent of the lender or estate agent. When you have received the advice ask for a quotation for remedial work and use this to negotiate a price reduction on the sale of the house.

Neighbourhood research

When you have found a property you are interested in you need to conduct some neighbourhood research. You need to know whether you, your family or your tenants would be happy living in the area. You should speak to neighbours either by knocking on doors or by visiting nearby businesses such as shops and pubs.

Get to know the local groups and community involvement this will help to decide if you, your family or tenants could integrate. Visit the neighbourhood at different times of the day and walk around the area not just drive. You will be able to check out the local facilities and amenities. Visit schools, colleges and universities and get a feel for the facilities and talk to teachers and other parents to see if they are suitable. Make sure there are enough entertainment and leisure facilities especially if you are looking to move tenants in.

Home information pack

This pack will contain information on property provided by the selling agent. It will contain the energy performance certificate, local searches, evidence of title proving the seller owns the property and a statement of the ownership type such as leasehold, freehold and commonhold.

Other information may include the condition of property, guarantees and warranties, home use and content forms and a legal summary of the documents. This information is not compulsory to the pack. Use this home information pack to make sure all the compulsory elements are correct and question the selling agent on anything that is not clear.

Survey

If you have reached the stage that you want to buy the property then you should arrange a survey. The survey can alert you to any problems with the property that could influence you to pull out of the purchase. There are different types of survey you can arrange:

Homebuyer's Report

This is a suitable survey for properties built within the last 150 years. The report will cover major and minor faults and any issues with the structure of the building including damp tests. However, this survey will not check underneath carpets, the wiring or any difficult to access areas. As certain conditions may be missed and you are in any doubt a structural survey may be the better option. The survey will cost in the region of £300-£450.

Full Structural Report
This survey for residential properties is more comprehensive and includes all major and minor faults with the property and information on the construction of the property. It is suitable for older properties, listed buildings, empty properties and houses that have been renovated or altered. The report will be very detailed and you should seek clarification on any issue with the surveyor. The surveyor may advice you to contact a specialist to provide expert advice on a problem with the building. Some problems may be too expensive or extremely difficult to rectify and this could ultimately mean you deciding to pull out of the purchase. Although you will lose your money on the survey it may be a wise decision to walk away from the property and find another property with fewer problems. A full structural survey will cost in the region of £600-£1000.

Sourcing repossessed property

We have looked at where to find repossessed property with the two most common methods through auction or from an estate agent.

Buying at auction

As stated earlier you should look at out for phrases in the auction catalogue such as 'By order of the mortgage' or 'By order of...Building Society'. There will be a guide price that the property will be expected to sell at. The lender who may be selling the property may set a reserve price as well. The lender's objective is to get the best price possible for the property to recover the debt owed by the mortgagee.

Before the property goes to auction it is possible to make an offer on the property. If the lender accepts the offer the property may be taken off the catalogue. However, this is usually when contracts have been exchanged.

It is recommended that you should visit and view the property before making any kind of bid at auction. Contact the auction house who will book you in for a day and time to visit the property. When viewing the property go through your checklist and avoid any potential pitfalls. You will need to arrange a surveyor to have a look at the property and advise you on any structural problems. You will need the service of a solicitor or conveyancer before the auction to look at all the legal paperwork on the property. The solicitor/conveyancer will inform you of any issues that you need to be aware of. You must also arrange your finance before the auction this includes having enough cash for the deposit and a mortgage from a lender. Mortgages will include fees for administration and a possible re-inspection fee where the lender will withhold part of the loan until agreed repairs are carried out.

You should prepare yourself well for the day of the auction as detailed below:

- Make sure you have enough funds for at least a ten percent deposit
- Make sure a mortgage agreement is in place for the auction
- Check survey reports to make the sure the property is structurally okay and that there are no expensive repairs
- Talk to your solicitor about the purchase to avoid problems
- Check the legal documents available from the auctioneer
- Have your auction catalogue with you at the auction this forms part of the legal contract. Both you and the lender (seller) will sign their copy and will be exchanged on purchase. The signed copy will be a receipt.
- Check the location of the venue and research any problems with traffic and road works that could delay you.
- Take the following to auction
    - Two forms of identification
    - Your deposit (cheque, cash, bankers draft)
    - Auction catalogue
    - Solicitors details
- Cover the cost of the auction fees which could be for administration or 'contract documentation'.

Before bidding begins read the 'announcement' sheet and listen out for any alterations to the property you are going to bid on. Through your background research and your available finances you will have an idea of the price you are willing to bid up to. Write this figure on a piece of paper. When bidding begins on your property don't immediately jump in with a bid. Wait and listen for anyone else to start. An experienced bidder will do this in the hope that the auctioneer will lower the starting price if there are no bidders. Once a bid comes in, start to join in with the bidding process. Bid slowly and don't look too keen.

Do not worry about accidental bids as an auctioneer will ask for bids to be made clearly by raising a hand or the auction catalogue. If the price has gone too high make it clear to the auctioneer that you no longer intend to bid by shaking your head. Once your bid has been accepted this becomes the 'exchange of contracts' and you cannot pull out of the purchase.

You can now bid without attending the auction either by telephone, internet or by using someone from the auction team. You will need to arrange this bidding process at least two days before the auction date.

Buying through an estate agent

When you have found a repossessed property through an estate agent the first stage in the buying process is to make an offer. When making an offer through an estate agent make sure it is put through to the lender. Some estate agents may tell you that the price is non-negotiable to get the best price but many lenders will negotiate.

Your research and price analysis should give you an indication of the maximum price you would be willing to pay. Your first offer should be well below this price. The lender may well accept this offer, but estate agents may continue to advertise to invite higher offers.

If you can move quickly on the sale (cash buyer being an example) you may be able to convince the estate agent to withdraw the advertising. If advertising goes ahead then this could be a problem as a bidding war could begin.

The agent will advertise typically up to 14 days and will invite 'sealed bids'. This means all bids are valid until a specified date when the highest bidder gets the property. This advertisement is used when there is high interest. The alternative is for the agent to advertise for open bids up until the exchange of contracts.

A sealed bid will be made in writing and you should decide on how much you are willing to offer. Only one bid can be made by each bidder in a sealed bidding process. The buyer should be in a position to complete the purchase in 28 days. I f you fail to win the bid you should still stay in contact with the estate agent. There are many cases where the highest bidder pulls out of the purchase having realised they have bid too much.

In an open bid process the estate agent will take offers from interested buyers and will go back and forth to see if a further bid is made if the previous bid is beaten. A bidding war may break out and the price could be driven considerably higher.

Below are key points to illustrate successful bidding in both sealed and open bidding:

Sealed bids:
- Use your price analysis to work out how much to offer and estimate what rival bidders will offer
- Make sure finances are arranged
- Offer an odd amount such as £175,001 that may beat an offer of £175,000
- Make sure you can act quickly to complete the purchase
- Try and find out how many bidders are involved by talking to the estate agent

- Only use reputable estate agents (no questionable practices)

Open bids:
- Read local papers and be in regular contact with estate agents
- Make an offer as soon as the property is advertised
- You are more likely to be successful in less active times of the year such as Christmas
- Know the procedures and make regular contact with the agent, bid quickly as soon as a higher bid comes in

Always try to complete the sale as quickly as possible, as other bids maybe invited up to the exchange of contracts. You can ask for a letter from an estate agent confirming that the property will no longer be advertised to stop this. Once contracts are exchanged neither party can pull out of the transfer and are legally bound.

Conveyancing

Conveyancing starts when you make an offer on a property and ends when you receive the keys. A solicitor or conveyancer usually conducts the conveyancing process although it is possible for you to do this yourself (providing there is no mortgage).

Firstly you will need to find a solicitor if you are not doing the conveyancing yourself and instruct them to carry out the process for you.

The appointed solicitor will draw up a contract and engagement letter that will include the charges and deposits required. The solicitor will contact the seller's solicitor to confirm that they are instructed and request a copy of the draft contract, property details and title deeds.

Your solicitor will study the draft contract and raise any queries with the seller's solicitor. You will also be expected to read through the forms filled out by the seller and raise any queries with your solicitor. Always check the tenure of the home; if it is leasehold then confirm the length of the lease with the seller. Solicitors don't always check this and if the lease is less than 80 years then it can be costly to extend it.

The solicitor will carry out searches on the property to check for any legal issues that you should be aware of. There may be things not noted on the survey or by viewing that you should know about. The following legal searches will carried out:

- Local authority search such as a planned motorway nearby
- The title deeds checked and verified
- Checking for flood risks
- Water authority searches to find out how the property gets its water
- Chancel repair search where there may be a medieval liability for church repairs
- Location specific searches for example when there has been mining in the area
- Environmental searches if the site was previously a landfill or recycling site

Your solicitor will want to go through your mortgage offer if you require one and check the terms of the offer. They will also check to ensure that you have adequate financing in place for the deposit. A mortgage valuation will be required so that the mortgage lender knows that there is sufficient security against the loan.

You should have had your survey carried out and building insurance in place before the exchange of contracts.

Before signing the contract your solicitor needs to ensure that all enquiries have been returned satisfactory, fixtures and fittings are what you expected, a completion date has been agreed. The solicitor will need to agree on you the deposit to be transferred into his/her account, usually 10% of the value of the property.

You and the seller will agree on a date and time for when to exchange the contracts. Your solicitor will exchange the contracts for you. If you are in a chain the solicitor will only release the contract when other people in the chain agree to go ahead.

Once contracts are exchanged you are in a legally binding contract to buy the property. If you do not go through with the purchase you lose the 10% deposit. If the seller does not sell then you can sue the seller. The seller cannot accept another offer on the property.

Once the exchange has been completed you can then move into your new home.

What happens when somebody moves in?

Once you have completed the acquisition of the repossessed property you need to make sure it is safe and in suitable condition to live in. A property is sold as seen and the onus is on you to make sure the property is safe and in working order.

It is important that you view the property before buying and if you find any damage or deliberate sabotage you may negotiate a reduction in selling price or have the problems rectified. Also, before someone moves in you will need to reconnect all services to the property. This will require contacting service providers to open a new account.

Safety inspection of the property

When you have bought the property you should carry out a risk and safety assessment noting down all areas of damage or disrepair. This could be wiring and connection problems and issues with waste and heating. Many of these problems require an expert to spot so you need to consider the following tradespeople to carry out the assessment:

Electrical inspection

An electrician will assess the electrical safety of the property and will certainly be required if you don't know who carried out the electrical installations. The government has introduced new laws on electrical safety that state that any work on, or installing, electrical installations must be carried out by an approved electrical supplier.

Information on these standards can be found on the National Inspection Council for Electrical Installation Contracting (NICEIC) website www.niceic.org.uk. They also have a database of listed qualified electrical contractors. It is recommended that an electrical inspection of a home should be carried out every ten years.

Gas inspection

Before you decide to sell the property or move a tenant in, contact a registered contractor to check all gas installations and appliances. All work including, installations, inspections and remedial work should be carried out by a registered installer with the Council for

Registered Gas Installers (CORGI) who have the correct qualifications for the type of work. To find a registered installer use the CORGI database at www.trustcorgi.com.

Gas checks include the boiler, the gas hob and the gas fire. Some companies will offer discount if you have a gas and electrical inspection together and you may have the boiler serviced at the same time.

Portable appliance inspection
Any electrical item that can be moved while electrically supplied is a portable appliance. This includes refrigerators, freezers, electric lawn mowers, bathroom heaters, electric cookers and air conditioning units. If any of these have been left in the property then they should be tested by the electrician. You can find an approved contractor from the NICEIC.

Inspections for landlords
If you intend to use the property to let to tenants then Landlord and Tenants Act 1995 requires that landlords who have properties with short leases keep electrical installations in good repair and working order. As well as the first electrical inspection on the property a periodic inspection should be carried out with a copy of the inspection available to tenants.

The Consumer Protection Act 1987 also makes it an offence for any landlord who provides portable appliances that are electrically unsafe. Appliances should be inspected regularly by an NICEIC approved electrician. Legally gas safety inspections should be carried out annually as well as when you first purchase the property. The inspection has to be carried out by a CORGI registered contractor. A landlord's gas safety certificate is to be given to your tenants.

Utilities and services

There are various organisations that you will need to inform that you have ownership of the property and are responsible for the utilities. If a tenant moves in then you should give them details of the current suppliers.

When you legally complete on the property take meter readings of electricity, gas and water. You can use these dates for any disputes on services you have not used.

Contact your local distribution company to find out your electricity supplier. Contact the supplier and ask for the Meter Point Administration Service and inform them of your name, address and postcode. For gas suppliers call Transco's Meter Helpline 0870 608 1524 to get the name of your registered supplier.

Once you have found the companies supplying to the property write a letter to each of them. Include your name, address and the date that you moved in and also include your meter readings. Include contact details of the lender's (who sold the property) address or the selling agent and ask for all correspondence relating to the previous owner is addressed to them.

It may take several months before records are updated by the supplier and you will continue to get bills addresses to the previous owner. Legally you cannot open someone else's mail. What you can do is score through the address on the envelope, write on the front NOT KNOWN AT THIS ADDRESS RETURN TO SENDER and put it in a post box.

Some services may be disconnected due to the previous occupier not paying a bill. As long as pipes are in good order and you, or a tenant, can provide proof of the last address then there will be no problem reconnecting to the service provider. You can give 28 days' notice if you intend to change your supplier. Both the old and new supplier will need an accurate meter reading.

You may not be able to get a reconnection if pipes are damaged. If the pipes are in the house or within your boundaries then you are responsible for the cost to repair. If they are outside your boundaries as part of the mains, then responsibility is with the supplier. If there has been deliberate damage then the supplier may not pay for the cost and you may have to seek legal advice.

If the pipes are shared by neighbours, then all the neighbours should share the cost of the repair. If there has been deliberate damage then you may want to cover the cost yourself to maintain goodwill with the neighbours.

Local authorities

Tenants should inform the local authority in order to be included on the electoral register. Once they are on the electoral register credit agencies will be able to update their address and they should not have any problems with their credit rating. They will also need to contact the local authority that they have moved in for council tax purposes.

A tenant should give them the date that they moved in and inform them that you do not know the whereabouts of the previous owner. You yourself will need to contact the local council if you intend to move in tenants on a certain date. The council tax is charged daily from the date that a person moved in.

If nobody can move in straight away because the property needs work before it is habitable you are exempt from council tax for up to six months. If the property was empty six months before the date of completion then the exemption is exhausted and you will have to pay the tax.

Issues with living in a repossessed property

There could be problems if you decide to let a property rather than sell it straight away. Sometimes problems arise when a tenant moves in and they have been living in the property for some time. It is important to make tenants aware of the problems that can occur and that the tenants know their rights to be able to deal with them.

Problems can arise due to out of date information with credit agencies and organisations chasing debts left by previous occupants. It may be best to try and sort some of these issues out before you move a tenant into a property that was previously repossessed.

Updating details held by credit agencies

A credit rating will not be based on the property, but a tenant may have problems obtaining credit from a lender. This is because the lender checks the electoral register to confirm that the client lives at that address. A tenant may be refused credit if their name does not appear on the register. To rectify this problem you or the tenant has three options:

- Contact the local authority to inform the tenant has moved in
- The tenant asks the lender who they are borrowing from to check the electoral register on their previous address. They may need proof that they moved house and will need explain

that the house they have moved to was repossessed
- A tenant can show the lender several types of evidence that they live at their current address

The tenant can use a credit report from a credit agency to ascertain any problems such as inaccuracies and mistakes that may hinder any future credit.

Dealing with debt collectors

Despite informing organisations, debt collectors can still hassle tenants after they have moved in. They could also hassle you as the landlord of the property. Debt collectors may contact your tenant by telephone, letter or face-to-face. Debt collectors work on behalf of creditors but they are not bailiffs. They are not allowed to enter the house, seize possessions, harass or intimidate your tenants. If this happens either you or the tenant should report them to the police or contact the local authority's trading standards department.

It is important you keep records of your house purchase, the date a tenant moved in along with proof of your identity and a tenant's identity so that you can prove to debt collectors that you and the tenant do not personally owe the debt. You are not obliged to do this, unless you feel it will help your case. If the debtor continues to pursue the debt and does not accept that you or the tenant are not the debtor then, again, report to trading standards. A debtor can no longer send a demand when it is not certain the individual is the debtor. All collection activities must stop, if this is not the case then again report them.

The Data Protection Act

The Data Protection Act gives you the right to know what information is held about you. If you have any issue with which a company has held your personal information you should report it to the Information Commissioner's Office (www.ico.gov.uk) who will intervene.

This is useful if the company has inaccuracies with your information. The Act also allows individuals access to information held on a computer or a paper record. This is useful if you need to access a credit file if you are having problems obtaining credit.

The Freedom of Information Act

If you want to find out information held by public authorities that is not personal data, then you can make a request under the Freedom of Information Act. The request must be made in writing either by letter, fax or email stating your name and address and clearly stating the information you require. The authority has 20 working days to supply the information. The public authority will not breach the Data Protection Act or supply anything that could harm national security or affect commercial interests. An example of use would be if you required the local authority's policy on debt collectors.

Chapter Twelve: Assisted sales

As you are conducting your property searches using some of the other strategies we have talked about, you may come across owners who may require help in selling their property. The owner may have had offers that don't match the value they are looking for. They may have bought a property for £100,000 and are looking for substantial profit. They are not interested in a long-term agreement, such as a lease option, they want to sell now.

This presents an opportunity for an investor to take short-term control of the property in order to refurbish and sell quickly. Here is an example of the figures that could work for the investor.

Motivated seller wants a sale for:
£100,000

Property Market Value (after refurbishment):
£140,000

Refurbishing Costs:
£15,000

Profit:
£25,000

These figures present the opportunity for someone to come along and assist the seller with getting the property sold and make money in the process.

An agreement will need to be drawn up which will be similar to a lease option agreement but with a lot shorter period of time. This will grant the investor or trader the permission to refurbish the property and sell it within a certain time frame (six months would be typical). The property could be placed on the market with an estate agent or sold through an auction. The refurbishment has added value to the property getting to the maximum true market value.

Assisted sales can also suit a joint venture because you, as the investor or trader, may not have enough funds to carry out the refurbishment. Therefore, a business partner is required with the necessary funds to complete the refurbishment. The joint venture partner will want to see a return on this money and a share of the profits.

You will need to have a written agreement for the allocation of profits. Don't be surprised if you have to give up at least 50 percent of whatever profit is made on the sale.

Assisted sales have its own risk similar to the risk involved with lease options. The money put into the refurbishment could be at risk if the seller goes back on the agreement. Make sure everything that is agreed is written and signed by both parties.

Part Three: Setting up the business

This section will help you with setting up your business and putting resources together. You will understand what you need to start property dealing and how you can grow your business in the future. This is a business that can be run as a one man band but there may be a time when you need to employ other people, most likely on a part-time or ad-hoc basis. You can't do everything yourself.

You also need to consider how to put your team together to help you put deals together and carry out certain tasks to get a property deal from the offer stage to completion. I will also explain the tax treatment for property trading and list useful resources that will help you with your business and learn more beyond what this book teaches you.

Hopefully, you will know how to get organised and be more confident as you start to master your patch and find property deals.

Chapter Thirteen: Business structure

The beauty of starting this business is that you can bootstrap and not employ anyone other than yourself. You won't need to do PAYE and your accounting will be much simpler to work out. You should treat the venture as a micro-business and keep overheads low. As things start to build you then you can start thinking about employing people. It is important that before you setup the business that you register with a property redress scheme, as mentioned in Chapter Nine: Rent to Rent. You will also need an escrow system to hold finder fees, which should be released once a deal is completed. Insurance should also be a consideration. As a dealer, sourcer or trader you are in a position where you are advising an investor. Professional indemnity insurance is a must. You may want to add extra cover for legal costs.

Accounts and tax

A good accounting and landlord software package would be useful to keep track of multiple rooms and rent payments. It is likely that there will be a lot of time dealing with tenants and rooms, so having an accountant will take the tax and accounting work away. You may want to consider some software that will track expenditure for refurbishments and renovation work.

The office setup

The office can be set-up from home with very little overheads. The equipment needed will be a PC or laptop, internet broadband, a printer and a mobile phone or landline. That is all that is required and it is likely that you already have most of this technology already in your household. You can produce some of your marketing materials in house by using your own printer.

You might want to think about using a smartphone rather than an ordinary phone to help you communicate while you are out and about viewing property. You can use the phone to take pictures on viewings.

Using a lightweight laptop or tablet could be a good item of equipment if you want to go through figures with motivated sellers or investors. You can use spreadsheets and analysis software to calculate offers and deals.

Will I require any staff?

It is possible to run this business on your own at the start and just use contractors for getting each property refurbished. As the business grows and the portfolio of property grows it may be wise to employ staff. You may want to employ leaflet distributors to post leaflets through letter boxes.

You might think about employing a part-time cleaner to keep the properties tidy between lets and keep common areas attractive. Handymen and gardeners can be used on an ad-hoc contract basis rather than employed.

Should administrative duties become a burden then an administrator could be employed if the business is managed from an office rather than from home. Many small businesses are using virtual assistants on an hourly basis to help with administrative duties, a good option if you want to keep running the business from home.

Property manager

Should you build a substantial portfolio of rent to rent properties or you have a number of properties in your portfolio that have been let rather than sold, you may want to consider employing a property manager.

Whether you employ a property manager part-time or full-time will depend on your budget and the number of properties you have.

This is a good option if you want to focus on other investments and need the time. Perhaps you are a developer that needs time to concentrate on building projects; it would make sense to employ someone to take care of the management side of the business.

Chapter Fourteen: Managing a refurbishment

You are going to be overseeing refurbishment projects if you offer deal packaging, assisted sales and lease option agreements. Rent 2 Rent opportunities may also involve some basic decoration and furnishings to get the property ready for rental. A lot of refurbishments are going to be simple whereas properties that are a complete wreck are going to require good project management skills.

Planning

By doing thorough due diligence on the property you will have worked out what work needs to be done to get the property into shape. In order to plan your costs and work out what profit margin you could expect you will need to get quotes from your refurbishing team of trusted tradesmen.

You will also want to work out how long it will take to get the refurbishment finished and ready for the market. The key is organisation and not wasting time delay getting the property sold or let. You should have organised project plans for every room and the exterior of the property before researching supplies and labour required.

Always produce a schedule of works that can help prove the work that has been done to add value to a property.

Records and receipts

You should keep track of all of the spending and keep hold of the receipts. Good accounting will enable you to offset the expenses on your tax bill. Remember, any work that is carried out in order to maintain the property is tax deductible on income. Examples would include replacing an old carpet, repainting the walls or fixing a damaged bathroom.

Basically, if it involves restoring the property to its original condition then it is a repair. Work that is carried out in order to improve the property is a cost that should be offset against capital gains tax should you decide to sell. Either way, all work should be well documented or receipts kept as proof.

Receipts should include materials used and any tradesman and labour involved in the work. Contracts and schedules of work are also other good examples of evidence of the work carried out. You will want to keep strict control if you want to make sure there is profit left in a deal.

If you have done thorough work at the planning stage then you have the best chance of making money from the deal. Stick to your plan but have a contingency if there are unexpected costs.

Add value

Work can be carried out to improve the property and add value. You may increase the value of your property and the amount of rent you can achieve by adding an extra bedroom, bathroom or toilet. Perhaps a large room can be split into two or a loft conversion is possible.

There is also the possibility of knocking two small rooms into one. An extension could be added, especially if there is room at the rear of the property with garden space. Work such as a loft conversion or extension may require planning permission from the local council's planning department.

This can take time and it is wise to talk to a surveyor as well as the planning department to make sure there is a strong chance that you will get the permission for the work. The planning department will want to see plans for the work so an architect or construction company will be required to assist you in this process. Loft conversions can avoid planning permission if they are within certain size requirements.

Buy refurbish refinance

You may have a property that you want to refurbish to sell perhaps as a packaged deal or a joint venture but the market has taken a turn for the worse. You might not be able to sell the property right away due to price reduction or lack of interested buyers. Now you have the problem of money being tied in to the property.

Now that the property has been refurbished to an excellent standard with added value you can use this to pull out cash from the deal. This works through a straightforward purchase of a buy to let property with a deposit and a typical 75 percent loan to value mortgage. Once you have purchased the property you carry out the refurbishment costs and add value to the property.

With this added value, you look to re-mortgage the property at the new value and therefore be able to pull out the original deposit and costs. However, this strategy will only work with extensive refurbishment as you will need to prove the added value to the mortgage lender and a surveyor. Pictures of before and after and records of the schedule of works will help to prove the added value.

This is a useful strategy to build a portfolio quickly or move onto another project but you should leave money in the bank as a contingency just in case you don't get the re-valuation.

Chapter Fifteen: Putting a team together

I have already covered a little about who you will need in your team to be a successful property dealer but you have to find those team members. Finding good quality professionals is not easy and it can be stressful and costly if you end up with unreliable and poor quality work.

Contact details of the organisations I recommend to find professionals for your team are listed in the Resources chapter. Some of the recommendations are organisations that I have used myself and have been impressed with.

Your legal team

You want to find a solicitor that is comfortable with the conveyancing process and is, ideally, a property specialist. The solicitors I have used and recommend are *Premier Property Lawyers.* They are property lawyers and are an award-winning national company. I have used them a couple of times for investment property and they are excellent.

They make the whole process really easy. Instead of having to go into offices and having lots of meetings you do everything online. So if there is information and documents that they require then you upload them online via a password protected login portal. I think they are brilliant for both buying and selling houses.

I would also seek a professional advice from a solicitor if you are going to use one of the advanced techniques such as lease options and assisted sales. You are going to need correct paperwork drawn up and you won't be qualified to this on your own.

Your finance team

You are going to need a mortgage broker and a qualified accountant. Your mortgage broker needs to be able to find you the best mortgage products but also provide you with expert advice on what is the best product to choose for your investment.

For instance, you may want to find mortgage products that do not have an early redemption payment charge if you are planning to sell the property in the short-term. There are many mortgage brokers around but I recommend *The Mortgage Broker Ltd*. They are a network of professional and highly experienced mortgage brokers up and down the UK. The broker I was assigned to was really helpful and friendly and had sound knowledge having dealt with lots of investors and property traders in the past.

You are also going to need a qualified accountant to help you structure your business and make the most of your money through effective accounting techniques. Your accountant may not be a qualified tax advisor, so you might want to add a tax specialist to your team.

You could potentially lose a lot of money to taxation that you could otherwise save by using effective tax strategies.

Your refurbishment team

I cannot recommend anyone personally as you may be living in a different area to me. I can offer you advice on how to find reputable tradesman. For general builders or refurbishment specialists you should ask other people you know or anyone else who has had work done to their property. You can also look to local councils who may have a list of reputable tradesman.

I found my refurbishing company through the *Derbyshire Trusted Trader* scheme and there might be something similar in your region. For specialist trades like electrical work, plumbing and gas/heating you should take a look at the trade body sites who oversee the regulations and qualifications. I have listed the websites in the Resources chapter.

There may be times when it is worth contracting a surveyor, especially if the property goes beyond a basic refurbishment and is need of a small renovation. They may be able to give you pointers on where you could add value to the property.

Your sales team

By visiting your local high street you will find all the major estate agents in your area. It is worth visiting and talking to several estate agents before deciding on who you want to sell the property. They may offer different terms and commission rates so take your time deciding. Also, think about whether you could work with them well and that they have the ability to sell the property fast.

It could be trial and error so that after you have done a few deals and tried different estate agents you will know who the best is. It might be wise to choose an estate agent you have built a relationship with in sourcing good property deals so that you doing them a favour in return.

You can also use online agents like *Purple Bricks*. I have never used an online agent so I cannot vouch for whether this is a good way to sell property but it is another option.

You may also want to network with other property sourcers that may deal in property or strategies that are not your specialty. This could be a great way to trade and source leads and help improve the reputation of your business. You will truly be able to help a seller in any situation, even if you cannot directly provide a solution.

Your management team

You might want to employ a property manager if you decide to let a property and you don't want to manage it yourself. I have already mentioned the need for a property manager for Rent to Rent where, as your portfolio grows, you may have too much work to take on yourself.

It might be better to concentrate on sourcing good deals and going through the buying and refurbishing process, especially if you have never managed property before. Like estate agents, property managers and letting agents will be found on the high street in your local town. Again, you are going to have to find the best, or should I say cheapest, management fees. But don't let this be the only criteria.

Try to get recommendations from other people who have used the management service and talk to the agent to see whether you would get along. You will want a property manager who deals with tenant and maintenance issues quickly.

Chapter Sixteen: Tax treatment for a property dealer

The techniques I have covered in this book classifies as the activities of a property trader or dealer. The only exception would be rent 2 rent that may class as a rental business and therefore would have the tax treatment as an investor rather than a trader.

A property trader is someone who holds properties for short-term gain in a mannered and methodical way (as this book describes) as a full-time activity. If you go down the route of frequently buying houses as stock (bought by yourself or through joint venture) to be sold on then you are a trader or dealer.

You would still be classed as a dealer if you are using lease options as you are looking to make profit from the sale of the property with any rental income (from a tenant-buyer) being incidental income.

You will usually differ from a property developer because many of your properties may require no work at all in order to do a deal and sell on. If you do work on the property such as a full refurbishment then the tax treatment may become similar to that of a property dealer. It would be best to consult a tax adviser on this.

A property trader will have the following tax treatment:

- Profits from property sales should be taxed as trading profits and will therefore fall within the Income Tax regime.
- Any rents achieved may be treated as incidental trading income or may be treated under the special rules of property income

- There is no relief for Inheritance Tax or business property
- Long term assets are eligible for entrepreneur's relief, an example would be office premises
- You do not pay Capital Gains Tax (CGT) when you sell a property
- If you are trading as a company rather than as an individual then trading profits will fall within the Corporation Tax regime instead of income tax.

You may want to consult a tax adviser if a property requires a scheme of works to refurbish the property ready for sale.

If the work is classed as property development then register for the Construction Industry Scheme (CIS). Any contractors such as electricians, builders, plumbers, heating engineers and other tradesmen will be paid through the scheme for tax purposes. Tax is deducted at a special rate from payments to contractors and will be accounted for as like PAYE for employees in a business. The tax deductions will differ in rate depending on whether the sub-contractor is registered for CIS or not.

How you structure your business will depend on what works best for tax rates. You may want to consider operating as a company in order to avoid Income Tax rates that are higher than Corporation Tax rates. The Rent 2 Rent business would be best formed as a limited company to limit the financial and legal risk should the business go wrong. A limited company will also look more professional to landlords who require the service. The business will require £5000 minimum of start-up capital to cover refurbishments. More funds may be needed if you are going for upmarket tenants in expensive locations. The business activities are primarily property rentals this is not a property development business it does not require huge amounts of money to renovate the property to sell.

Chapter Seventeen: Resources

Tools to source property deals and conduct analysis

Below is a list of websites that you can use to conduct property deal analysis and search for potential deals.

Zoopla – www.zoopla.co.uk

Rightmove – www.rightmove.co.uk

Mouseprice.com – www.mouseprice.com

Nationwide House Price Index - www.nationwide.co.uk/about/house-price-index/headlines

Useful sites to source repossessed property

These websites will help you filter potential properties for investment. These properties are likely to be sitting empty and require refurbishment.

Repo List – www.repolist.co.uk

SDL Auctions – www.sdlauctions.co.uk (formerly Graham Penny)

Further learning for Rent to Rent

Below is a list of books and course that you should think about purchasing to continue your training in rent to rent management. Just reading books is not the best way to learn this property strategy, taking courses with rent to rent experts are going to give you more practical experience. Another step to take in your training is to 'shadow' a rent to rent manager. By following a rent to rent manager for a week or two you can get a chance to see what the job entails. Rent to rent management is very hands-on and you will have to deal with people. This may not suit every investor who may be more suited to a hands-off investment that doesn't require day-to-day involvement.

Useful books

Rent2Rent: Landlords, Agents, Tenants & The Legal Skills You Need To Consider by Taiwo Orishayomi

Rent to Rent: Getting Started Guide by Jacquie Edwards

The Successful HMO Landlord by Anthony Dixon
This is my own guide on managing HMO property, which could be handy for a Rent 2 Rent manager using the HMO business model. It is available on Amazon.

Courses

https://www.hmodaddy.com/rent-to-rent a course provided by Jim Haliburton who is a well-known expert in HMO lettings

https://www.renttorentacademy.co.uk/ a training academy for people wishing to start a rent to rent management business

Perhaps you like the management side of Rent 2 Rent and would like to start a property management company on standard management agreements. If so then you could consider getting a professional property management qualification. ARLA Propertymark provides courses in residential letting and property management at level two and three. www.arla.co.uk

Further learning for lease options

This book covers a basic introduction to lease options as it is not my area of expertise. You may want to do further learning as you become experienced in sourcing property.

Useful books

Dominate Your Ground by Mark I'anson — There is also a DVD pack available

Escape The Rat Race: With Property Lease Options by Barry Davies

Further learning by Anthony Dixon

My YouTube educational channel, Dixon Property Deals — Posting video content about property trading techniques, a more practical learning than just reading this book

UK Property Lettings — My book that teaches you about managing rental property

Useful sites to help you put together your property dealing team

Refurbishing

https://www.gassaferegister.co.uk/find-an-engineer/ for registered gas tradesmen

https://www.electricalsafetyfirst.org.uk/find-an-electrician/ for qualified electricians https://www.fmb.org.uk/ - the federation of master builders would be a good starting point to find qualified builders for large refurbishment projects

Legal

http://www.premierpropertylawyers.com/ a solicitor that I recommend for conveyancing

https://www.rics.org/uk/ the Royal Institute of Chartered Surveyors where you can find a surveyor

Finance

https://www.icaew.com/ a good place to start in searching for a qualified accountant

https://www.tax.org.uk/homepage the Charted Institute of Taxation will have a list of qualified tax advisers

Appendix I Sample lead form

Seller Lead Form

Name:……………………………………………...

Email:……………………………………………

Contact Phone Number:………………………………

Property Address:……………………………………..

…………………………………………………......

…………………………………………………......

Owner's Name:…………………………………….

Vacant or Occupied:…………………………………...

Property Description

Type of Property:……………………………………

Number of Bedrooms:………………………………….

State of the Property:…………………………………………………
………………

………………………………………………………………
………………………………

………………………………………………………………
……………………………….

………………………………………………………………
……………………………….

Heating system:……………………………………………

Utilities are on:………………………………………………………
……………..

What repairs would they do to live in the house:………………………………………………

………………………………………………………………
…………………………….....

………………………………………………………………
……………………………......

Seller's Motivation:

How long have they owned the house:……………………………………………………....

Why are they selling:………………………………………………………….
……………..

………………………………………………………………
…………………………….....

………………………………………………………………
…………………………………..

What is the asking price?
Valuation?…………………………………………………………..
……………………..

………………………………………………………………………
………………………………….

Existing Mortgage:

Is there a mortgage:…………………….

How much mortgage is left:……………………………………………………………..
……………………..

Is the mortgage in their name:……………………………………………………….
……

Willing to sell 25 per cent BMV:……………………………….

Appendix II Example buy to let analysis

Deal Address: 45 Example Street, Derby
Buy to let

Purchase Price:	£95,000
Finder's Fee:	£0
Legal Costs:	£1,000
Stamp Duty Tax:	£2,850
Finance Fee & Survey Costs	£500
Total Investment:	£99,350
Investment with deposit:	£28,100
Mortgage LTV:	75%
Mortgage Amount:	£71,250
Deposit Amount:	£23,750
Monthly Rent:	£550
Annual Gross Rent:	£6,600
Gross Yield:	7%
Management Fees	£500
Void Period	£450
MOE	£500
Annual Net Rent:	£5,150
Monthly Net Rent:	£429
Interest Rate:	2.50%
Annual Mortgage Cost:	£2,434
Monthly Mortgage Cost:	£203

Monthly Cashflow:	£226
Yearly Cashflow:	£2,716

Gross Yield:	7%
Net ROI on Cash Left In Deal:	9.66%

Printed in Poland
by Amazon Fulfillment
Poland Sp. z o.o., Wrocław